A Practical Guide to
Solar Photovoltaic Systems
for Technicians

P9-AFT-997

04178729

A Practical Guide to
Solar Photovoltaic Systems
for Technicians
Sizing, Installation and Maintenance

Jean-Paul Louineau

PRACTICAL ACTION
Publishing

OKANAGAN COLLEGE
LIBRARY
BRITISH COLUMBIA

Intermediate Technology Publications Ltd
trading as Practical Action Publishing
Schumacher Centre for Technology and Development
Bourton on Dunsmore, Rugby,
Warwickshire CV23 9QZ, UK
www.practicalactionpublishing.org

© ETC Foundation and Jean-Paul Louineau, 2008

First published in English, 2008
First published in French, 2001

ISBN 978 1 85339 659 5

All rights reserved. No part of this publication may be reprinted or reproduced or utilized in any form or by any electronic, mechanical, or other means, now known or hereafter invented, including photocopying and recording, or in any information storage or retrieval system, without the written permission of the publishers.

A catalogue record for this book is available from the British Library.

Jean-Paul Louineau has asserted his right under the Copyright Designs and Patents Act 1988 to be identified as author of this work.

Since 1974, Practical Action Publishing has published and disseminated books and information in support of international development work throughout the world. Practical Action Publishing (formerly ITDG Publishing) is a trading name of Intermediate Technology Publications Ltd (Company Reg. No. 1159018), the wholly owned publishing company of Intermediate Technology Development Group Ltd (working name Practical Action). Practical Action Publishing trades only in support of its parent charity objectives and any profits are covenanted back to Practical Action
(Charity Reg. No. 247257, Group VAT Registration No. 880 9924 76).

Photo credits:
Jean-Paul Louineau, Alliance Soleil and Sylvain Charmoy, Systèmes Solaires.

Printed by Cambrian Printers on 100% recycled paper.

Published in association with

ETC Energy/TTP
PO. Box 64
3830 AB Leusden
Pays-Bas
Tel. : + 31 (0) 33 432 60 00
Fax: + 31 (0) 33 494 07 91
Email: energy@etcnl.nl
www.etc-international.org

Alliance Soleil
Jean-Paul Louineau
74, Avenue de L'Isle de Riez
85270 Saint Hilaire de Riez - France
Tel. : + 33 (0) 2 51 54 19 06
Fax: + 33 (0) 2 51 54 19 06
Email: alliance.soleil@wanadoo.fr
www.alliancesoleil.com

For information on the French version refer enquiries to

Fondation Énergies pour le Monde
146, rue de l'Université
75007 Paris - France
Tel. : + 33 (0) 1 44 18 00 80
Fax: + 33 (0) 1 44 18 00 36
Email: fondem@energies-renouvelables.org
www.energies-renouvelables.org

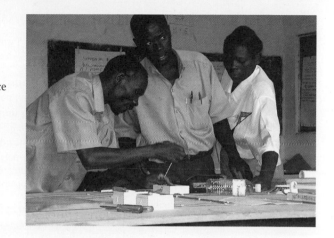

This publication is often used for technical training courses. In the event that you would like to organise such a training course, please contact ETC Energy/TTP to receive information and assistance.

Translation or modifications: in order to avoid unnecessary exercises and unintentional errors, or to make suggestions to improve the information contained within, please contact ETC Energy/TTP, before any translations or modifications.

Whilst the greatest care has been taken to verify the information contained in this document, neither the publisher nor the author can be held responsible for any damages resulting from the application of methods explained in this book.

Contents

Preface

We are proud to present the first English edition of the *Practical Guide to Solar Photovoltaic Systems: Sizing, Installation and Maintenance*. Containing practical advice that is easy to implement, it is the ideal tool for every promoter and user of solar systems.

It has been designed for use in the field in the same way as a screwdriver or multimeter. Its place is in the toolbox and not in the office! For this reason, it has been baptised the Paper Tool by its author Jean-Paul Louineau.

This paper tool is an integral part of a series of complete training tools by the same author, including a training manual for trainers. These documents have been used in vocational technical schools in several African countries and elsewhere.

First published in French, men and women in English-speaking countries now have access to this complete and practical manual. We hope that it will facilitate the sustainable use of solar systems and that the lives of many people in isolated sites will be improved by its dissemination.

We wish to thank Jean-Paul Louineau for his excellent work in creating this book, a manual necessary for the proliferation of energy systems which capitalise on the solar resources available everywhere and avoiding the use of imported combustibles and the increase of greenhouse gases.

We also wish to thank the ETC Foundation, ETC Energy / Technical Training Program, the French Environment and Energy Management Agency (ADEME), Alliance Soleil sarl and Practical Action Publishing, for their contributions to this publication.

Ms Willeke Parmentier
ETC Energy, TTP, July 2008

The author wishes to thank the team of readers created for this edition: Bernard Chabot (Ademe, France), Sylvain Charmoy (Democratic Republic of Congo), Emmanuel Goy (France), Kathleen Glancey (France), Yves Maigne (France), Willeke Parmentier (The Netherlands), Chris Purcell (South Africa), Voahirana Randriambola / Eric Huguot Raharisoa (Madagascar) and Djibril Semega (Mali).

 This symbol marks important warnings in the book.

1. Objective

The objective of this guide is to provide simple, direct and practical advice for the success and development of solar energy entrepreneurs (including salespeople, retailers and installers) in the field.

It proposes clear methods and advice to:

- evaluate the energy needs of clients and users,

- determine the appropriate size of small solar systems,

- estimate the prices of such systems,

- select and purchase quality components,

- ensure the marketing of solar systems as well as other services for clients,

- install, maintain and repair the solar systems, and

- inform and advise current and future solar system users.

For those who wish to obtain further information about solar systems, a list of references and websites is provided at the end of the manual.

This book seeks to be a necessary tool, as important for technicians and users as a screwdriver or a multimeter. It should be used in the field accompanied by any technical documentation provided by the manufacturers and suppliers of the material to be installed, repaired or maintained. The aim is to ensure the sustainability and quality of installations, the satisfaction of users and at the same time the success of solar entrepreneurs.

© JPL

The success of solar entrepreneurs depends primarily on their ability to satisfy their clients. This guide will help them in this mission.

2. Units of measure and basic formulae for electricity and energy

Units of measure

© JPL

• Hour	(h)	Unit of measure for **Time**		
• Volt	(V)	Unit of measure for **Voltage**	(V)	= (W) / (A)
• Ampere	(A)	Unit of measure for the intensity of **Current**	(A)	= (W) / (V)
• Ampere-hour	(Ah)	Unit of measure for the **Capacity** of a battery	(Ah)	= (A) x (h)
• Watt	(W)	Unit of measure for **Power**	(W)	= (Wh) / (h)
• Watt-hour	(Wh)	Unit of measure for the quantity of **Energy** (1 kWh = 1 000 Wh)	(Wh)	= (W) x (h)

Principal formulae

In the case of alternating current (AC)   **Units**
- **Power (P)**   = Voltage x Current x Power factor   → $P = U \times I \times \cos \varphi$ (W) = (V) x (A)

In the case of direct current (DC)   **Units**
- **Power (P)**   = Voltage x Current   → $P = U \times I$ (W) = (V) x (A)
- **Energy (E)**   = Power x Time   → $E = P \times Time$ (Wh) = (W) x (h)
- **Efficiency (η)*** = P out / P in   → $\eta = Po / Pi$ (%) = (W) / (W)

Formulae   Examples

$P = U \times I$	The power of a 9 V radio using a 1.5 A current is: $P = 9\ V \times 1.5\ A = 13.5\ W$
$E = P \times Time$	If a radio functions for 6 hours, the energy consumed is: $E = 13.5\ W \times 6\ h = 81\ Wh$

*All the terms in green may be found in the glossary.

$I = P / U$	An 8 W lamp powered with 12 V consumes a current of the following intensity: $I = 8 \text{ W} / 12 \text{ V} = 0.666 \text{ A}$
$P = E / \text{Time}$	A lamp that consumes 16 Wh in 2 hours has a power of: $P = 16 \text{ Wh} / 2 \text{ h} = 8 \text{ W}$
$E = U \times I \times \text{Time}$	After functioning for 2 hours, the consumption of this lamp will be: $E = 12 \text{ V} \times 0.666 \text{ A} \times 2 \text{ h} = 16 \text{ Wh}$
$C = E / U$	The lamp consumed: $C = 16 \text{ Wh} / 12 \text{ V} = 1.33 \text{ Ah}$
$Pi = Po / \eta$	A 50 W AC TV powered by an inverter whose efficiency is 75 %, needs: $Pi = 50 \text{ W} / 0.75 = 66.6 \text{ W (DC)}$

Units used specifically for solar energy

- **Watt/m²**: measures the instantaneous power (irradiance from the sun) received on one square metre of earth. *For example, the maximum is 1000 W/m² at noon on a sunny day. If the weather is inclement (clouds, rain, mist, etc.), the instantaneous power will be less than 1000 W/m².*

- **kWh/m²/day**: measures the energy (daily irradiation) that one square metre of earth receives from the sun during one day. *For example, in Marrakech, Morocco, on a yearly basis, the average daily irradiation is estimated to be 4.9 kWh/m² per day on a horizontal plane and 5.4 kWh/m² on a plane inclined to 40 degrees from the horizontal.*

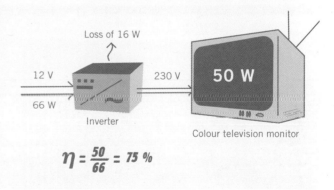

$$\eta = \frac{50}{66} = 75 \text{ %}$$

Colour television monitor

- **Wp (Watt peak)**: refers to the maximum power which a solar photovoltaic (PV) module can produce in optimal conditions of irradiance and temperature (1000 W/m² at 25 °C **solar cell temperature**).

13

3. Introduction to small solar photovoltaic systems

3.1. Definition

A small solar system is the complete set of equipment used in converting sunlight into electricity for a practical purpose, such as lighting or powering appliances like a radio, a television and various other electrical devices. Small solar systems are not larger than a few hundred watt peak (Wp). Such systems generally supply a nominal voltage in direct current (DC) of 12 V for systems up to 250 Wp, and of 24 V for systems greater than 250 Wp. The voltage level can be adapted to the needs of the electrical appliances. Some loads require a voltage supply less than 12 V or 24 V. Furthermore, others function in alternating current (AC) and need a voltage of 230 V AC (in exceptional cases 115 V AC).

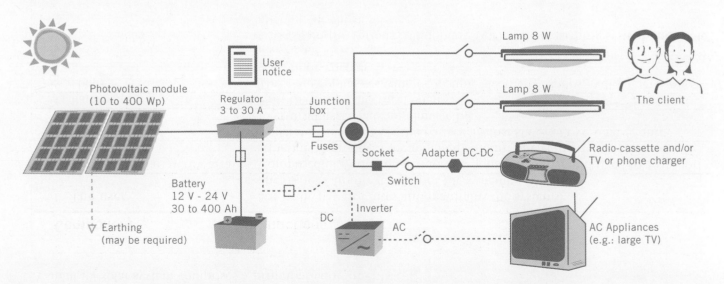

A small PV solar system comprises **5 principal components**:

Component	Functions
1 The user	She or he pays for, uses and maintains the systems. She or he is an integral part of the system!
2 Photovoltaic array (PV array)	Composed of photovoltaic modules joined together and fixed to a support structure, it produces the required amount of electricity.
3 Regulator	Apparatus that protects the battery against states of **overcharge** and **over-discharge** that can damage it.
4 Battery	Unit that stores electrical energy.
5 Loads	These are appliances which consume electricity: lamps, radio, television, cell-phone charger…
Cables	Cables join the various components (includes an earthing system and cable attachment clips).
Adapter	Unit that adapts the DC voltage from the battery to the DC voltage required by the load if it is higher or lower.
Inverter	Unit that converts direct current into alternating current (DC into AC).

3.2. Advantages and limitations of solar systems

Principal advantages	Principal limitations
✓ Low running costs: no more need for kerosene, candles or dry-cells.	✗ High purchase cost.
✓ System longevity: good quality PV modules can last for more than 20 years.	✗ Batteries are the weakest component of the system and necessitate a rigorous maintenance schedule.
✓ Low overall maintenance compared to the majority of energy systems using conventional sources of energy such as generators.	✗ System performance is dependent on respect for operating instructions and regular maintenance by the user which, although minimal, must be carried out regularly.
✓ Minimal user maintenance (requires cleaning the modules and checking the electrolyte level in the batteries regularly).	✗ User-training is required for maintenance and operation of the system.
✓ Less expensive in the long run than dry-cells for powering radios and cassette players.	✗ The user must carefully monitor his or her energy consumption.
✓ Easily upgraded (by adding modules, lights, etc.).	✗ The amount of energy provided by the system is limited by the number of PV modules installed.
✓ Produces a light of superior quality to that of candles or hurricane lamps.	✗ Cannot power big loads such as an electric iron, electric kettle or a large refrigerator (at the risk of over-sizing the installation).
✓ Easy and reliable usage (avoids the risk of fire from candles or hurricane lamps).	✗ PV modules are liable to theft unless proper security measures are taken during installation (for example, judicious choice of location and special materials such as self-breaking screws).
✓ Minimal risk of electric shock.	
✓ Silent.	✗ Renewing or replacing system components is rare but can be costly.
✓ Emits no toxic fumes or smoke.	

3.3. Safety and environment issues

Solar systems do not present any particular safety or environmental hazards. However, they should be considered as potentially dangerous, like any other source of electricity with a similar voltage.

- Batteries represent the greatest safety hazard. When **'vented' batteries** are used, care should be taken as the electrolyte acid is extremely corrosive and the hydrogen emitted is flammable and explosive. In **'sealed' batteries** the electrolyte is often in gel form and enclosed in the battery casing thus presenting less of a safety hazard. In both cases, particular attention must be paid to keeping the battery casing intact (refer to **section 7**).

- What to do with used batteries and fluorescent tubes?

    - Used batteries should be returned to the manufacturer for recycling (the lead is recycled to make new batteries).

    - Fluorescent tubes should be returned to large towns for recycling (they contain mercury which is a highly polluting substance).

4. The client: meeting his or her needs

The client or the user will pay for the system or pay for the use and maintenance of the system. He or she will use the system and make known his or her satisfaction or dissatisfaction about its performance. Like an automobile driver who drives his or her car with care in order to keep up its performance and limit its costs, the solar system user must do the same, **but can only do so if he or she knows or has been taught the optimal use of the system**.

The user will tell others of the advantages of solar systems. He or she will become a promoter of solar systems if his or her needs have been well satisfied.

Satisfying the needs of a client depends on the know-how (technical and commercial) as well as the integrity and honesty of the solar technician / entrepreneur.

Adding up to success:

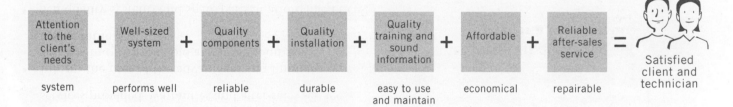

| Attention to the client's needs | + | Well-sized system | + | Quality components | + | Quality installation | + | Quality training and sound information | + | Affordable | + | Reliable after-sales service | = | Satisfied client and technician |
| system | | performs well | | reliable | | durable | | easy to use and maintain | | economical | | repairable | | |

Hence, it is essential to:

- Take time to listen to the client in order to identify and quantify his or her needs.

- Clearly present the range of systems on offer in terms of services provided, warranties and after-sales service.

- Inform the user of the advantages and limitations of solar systems in order to avoid any disappointments (using **table** 3.2).

- Sell quality systems and spare parts at affordable prices.

- Install reliable and long-lasting systems with the utmost care.

- Train and inform the user about the system during installation and at other major stages in the life of the system such as during servicing and repair visits.

- Remain available and accessible to the user – a locally based technician is an advantage.

- Finally, create and maintain good relations with the user.

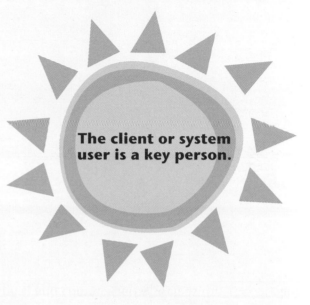

The client or system user is a key person.

There is nothing worse than to hear a client complaining 'my solar system is not capable of doing what the technician said it would'.

Becoming a serious entrepreneur means being clear and honest with the client: your clients will be satisfied and grow in number.

4.1. Sizing to sell solar systems

The sizing of a system has a direct effect on the price, quality and sustainability of the solar system.
It is a crucial step BEFORE any installation.

The principle for sizing is simple: finding the right balance between the energy **produced** by the modules and the energy **consumed** by the loads.

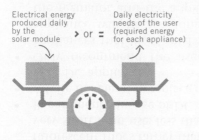

Electrical energy produced daily by the solar module **> or =** Daily electricity needs of the user (required energy for each appliance)

The size and composition of a system depends on:
- the energy consumed by each load every day (E = P x Time);
- the irradiation of the site i.e. the amount of solar energy received daily and its seasonal variations over the year;
- the energy efficiency of all the components of the system (battery, appliances, etc.);
- the availability of equipment on the local market (type and size of modules, batteries, lamps, etc.).

The process of sizing a system should be carried out in *5 consecutive steps*:
1. **Evaluation of the energy needs** to be met (through discussion and negotiation with the client in order to define the services to be provided).
2. Sizing of the solar module(s).
3. Sizing of the battery or batteries.
4. Choice of regulator.
5. Sizing of cables and electrical protection equipment.

Large energy requirements will increase the size and cost of the system!

Two examples of sizing using a *'simplified sizing procedure form'* are shown in the annexes as demonstrations: **Annex 1** shows a small system in DC and **Annex 2** a system with an inverter.

Use the *'blank simplified sizing procedure form'* proposed in **Annex 3**, to size each new solar system.

Energy efficient components will reduce the size of the system and often its cost!

Hints for step 1: Evaluating energy needs

- Ask the client which types of appliances she or he wishes to use (lighting, radio, etc.). Determine the average amount of time the appliances will be used each day, and if there are needs that vary according to the seasons.

Principle of minimal energy use

- Define needs by priority, arrange them by hierarchy and then evaluate the financial capacity of the client to meet such needs.
- Limit the number and type of appliances according to the power and energy that can be provided by a solar system.

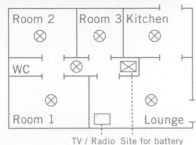

- Define with the client the ideal location of the appliances according to the activities planned in each room or site.

Principle of energy efficiency

- Recommend the most energy efficient appliances available for example, fluorescent tubes rather than incandescent light bulbs (except in the case of very short term use: less than 5 minutes per day).
- Recommend the use of DC appliances.
- Advise the client to replace old AC appliances that consume too much power with DC appliances.
- Only recommend the use of an inverter if the client possesses recent appliances that work solely on AC and/or if the cable length to reach the appliance will be too long (for example more than 20 metres between the regulator and the appliance. In any case, always calculate the voltage drops).

To be preferred !

To be avoided !

Principle of rigour

- Keep in mind the possible evolution of a client's needs over time.
- Always use the *'simplified sizing procedure form'* (see **Annex 3**).

Whenever possible, the sizing should be verified by the supplier or manufacturer of the PV equipment.

In cases where energy consumption varies greatly from day to day (for example heavy use of appliances at the weekends) or from season to season (for example during harvesting) consult a supplier to verify your sizing proposal.

Hints for step 2: choosing the irradiation figure

The solar module must receive sufficient energy to satisfy electricity needs throughout the period of use, especially during the less sunny months. Hence, seasonal variations must be taken into account.

	The Netherlands	The south of France	North African Countries	Sahel Countries	Central Africa	East Africa	Vietnam
Month with least sunshine	0.45	1.5	4.0	4.8	4.0	4.5	4.3
Month with most sunshine	4.9	7.0	6.5	7.0	5.5	7.0	6.0
Annual average	2.7	4.2	5.0	6.5	5.0	5.5	4.9

Examples of irradiation demonstrating seasonal variations (in kWh/m^2.day on a horizontal surface)
NOTE: these values are only indicative. They should not be used for sizing.

- Ensure that the irradiation figure (**kWh/m^2/day**) used is that of the **least sunny month for the period** when the solar system is to be used. The least sunny period in Europe is winter (e.g.: 1.7 kWh/m^2/day for a module inclined to 60°). In Africa, the least sunny period may be the rainy or dry season depending on the region (e.g.: 4.0 kWh/m^2.day for a module inclined to 20°).

- Irradiation figures may be obtained from government institutions such as the Ministry of Energy or National Meteorological Centres, from PV suppliers and from various Internet Sites (refer to **section 15**).

- **Ideally, you should study monthly irradiation values for several levels of inclination** (e.g.: horizontal, 15°, 30°, 45°, 60° and 75°). These values will help to determine the angle at which the module should be inclined, and the corresponding irradiation value to use for sizing.

  - Irradiation values on the horizontal plane will be sufficient for countries with latitudes between 0 and +/– 10° (near the equator). In such cases, the module will be installed at a very small degree of inclination (10° from the horizontal).

  - In countries where the latitude is greater than 10°, the module will often be inclined to an angle equal to the latitude of the site in order to receive the maximum irradiation throughout the year, or to an angle slightly greater (latitude + 10° or latitude + 20°) to receive maximum irradiation during the least favourable months.

    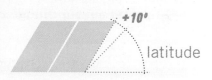

- When the irradiation value is not known for a given site, it can be estimated from known values of surrounding sites. For example, you need to determine the irradiation value to use for the village of Kelle in Senegal, but no data exists for this site. The values given below for the sites of Dakar and Saint-Louis allow one to estimate that for the site of Kelle, the minimal monthly irradiation will be 4.02 kWh/m2/day (this is the average between 3.76 and 4.28).

	Saint-Louis (Senegal)	Dakar (Senegal)
Distance from Kelle	160 km	200 km
The least sunny month (December)	3.76	4.28
The most sunny month (April)	6.42	6.70
Yearly average	5.21	5.44

Source: DASTPVPS / SOLARIRR.INS – Values in kWh/m²/day on a horizontal plane

- Once the irradiation value has been estimated, use the **'simplified sizing procedure form'**, to calculate the needed peak power of the solar panel.

4.2. Pricing a solar system...Making a quotation

Once a solar system has been sized and the components selected, it is possible to calculate the cost price and the selling price.

Calculating the sale price, or making a quotation, should be carried out in four consecutive steps:

1. List the components and evaluate their cost.

2. Calculate the installation costs, including labour and transportation costs.

3. Calculate the cost price of the system, or the price at which the entrepreneur pays for the system.

4. Calculate the sale price, or the cost price plus the profit margin. This is the price that will be paid by the client.

In your quotation, propose an annual maintenance visit for a given fee, renewable each year.

A *'quotation procedure form'* is provided in **Annex 4**. It has been filled in for demonstration purposes. The component prices are from the local market in Dakar, Senegal in 2008 (converted to Euros). A blank form is provided in **Annex 5**.

4.3. How to sell a correctly-sized system

- The system may end up being too expensive for the client. In this case make another quotation reducing the energy needs. Ensure that the client understands that the proposed system, while providing less energy, will still give satisfaction by providing advantages and more convenience than is experienced by a client without a solar system.

- Estimate the sale price of the battery and ensure that the client will have the means to replace the battery in a few years time. If that seems improbable, reduce, if possible, the needs of the client to obtain a more affordable battery.

- Propose two options for the batteries: solar batteries or car batteries. Always propose to sell new batteries, never used batteries.

- Explain that quality has a cost, especially if you sense that the client has knowledge of less expensive solar systems elsewhere. Such systems are likely to have been poorly designed or of doubtful quality (refer to **section 10**).

© JPL

The special case of 'very small' systems (10 to 30 Wp)

If the client does not have the means to buy a sufficiently large solar panel to power all the appliances desired, you can:

- Advise him or her to limit the amount of time the appliances will be used and to recharge the battery in town centres during the least sunny months when the panel will not fully charge the battery.

- Encourage him or her to buy a supplementary solar panel as soon as possible before the battery is rendered useless.

- It may be wise to advise the purchase of a more powerful panel (for example: two 14 Wp panels instead of one), rather than the purchase of a regulator. With panels greater than 30 Wp, a regulator is strongly advised.

25

5. Photovoltaic modules

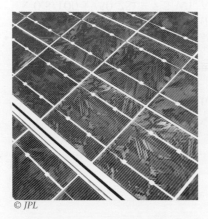

© JPL

Photovoltaic modules directly convert sunlight into DC electricity using solar cells.

The maximum power or output of a module is indicated in Watt peak (Wp). This is the power that a module will produce in optimal conditions of full sunshine (1000 W/m^2) and with a cell temperature of 25°C. Hence, a 60 Wp module can produce a maximum of 60 W in full sunshine at noon.

The amount of electricity produced from a PV module is easily calculated from its peak power, the daily irradiation value in the plane of the module and an average performance coefficient (estimated to be 0.60 for small systems with batteries). For example, if a module of 60 Wp receives a daily irradiation of 4.5 kWh/m^2, it will produce: 60 x 4.5 x 0.60 = 162 Wh/day.

Principal characteristics:

• **Peak power (Pp)**	**Pp**	For example, 7, 14, 60 to 160 Wp per module
• **Short circuit current (A)**	**Isc**	For example, 3.65 A for a 60 Wp module
• **Open circuit voltage (V)**	**Uoc**	For example, 20.7 V for a 60 Wp module
• Possibility of various output voltages		For example, 12 V or 24 V

• MOST COMMON TECHNOLOGIES:	*Lifetime*	*Manufacturer warranty*	
Monocrystalline silicon	15 to 30 years	10 to 30 years	Uniform dark blue cells
Polycrystalline silicon	15 to 30 years	10 to 25 years	Blue with reflection pattern cells
Amorphous silicon	5 to 20 years	5 to 10 years	Brown coloured cells

Other considerations:

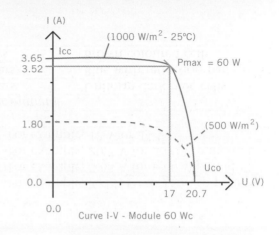

Curve I-V - Module 60 Wc

- Uoc is almost constant whatever the irradiance level (W/m2). Uoc varies between 0.5 et 0.7 V for each cell (for example, a module with 36 cells has an open circuit voltage Uoc of 36 x 0.6 = 21.6 V)

- Isc is directly proportional to the surface area of the cells (for example, a module with 36 cells each 10 cm x 10 cm, will have an Isc twice as large as a module composed of the same number of cells each 10 cm x 5 cm).

- Isc and power output are almost directly proportional to the irradiance received on a module:

EXAMPLE OF TYPICAL BEHAVIOUR	IRRADIANCE (W/m²)	OPEN CIRCUIT VOLTAGE Uco (V)	SHORT CIRCUIT CURRENT Isc (A)	POWER OUTPUT (W)
	100 (grey clouds at noon)	15	0.36	6
PV module 60 Wp	500 (white clouds at noon)	19	1.80	30
	1000 (clear sky at noon)	20	3.65	60

- At temperatures greater than 25°C (temperature of the cell itself), power output will decrease by 0.5% for each degree rise in temperature of the PV module (e.g.: at 50°C, the output of a 60 Wp module will decrease by 60 x 0.5/100 x (50-25) = 7.5 W). A PV module will always produce a bit less than its peak power, especially in hot climates.

6. Charge regulator

© JPL

The main function of a charge regulator is to protect the battery against states of overcharge and over-discharge, which will help to lengthen the life of the battery. The indicators on the regulator give valuable information about the functioning of the system.

Principal characteristics:

• Maximum current accepted from the PV array	between 3 and 30 A
• Maximum current deliverable to the load	between 3 and 30 A
• Low battery voltage indicator	LED, voltmeter or audible signal
• Solar charge indicator	LED or ammeter
• Voltage threshold for charging	*For example, high threshold* (module connected) *For example, low threshold* (module disconnected)
for a vented battery	14.5 V at 25 °C 12.8 V at 25 °C
for a sealed battery	14.1 V at 25 °C 12.8 V at 25 °C
• Voltage threshold for discharge	
for a vented battery	For example, between 10.5 and 11.9 V
for a sealed battery	For example, between 11.4 and 11.9 V
• Regulation type	With relay (all or nothing), Pulse with modulation (PWM) charging
• Reset (when battery voltage increases to a sufficient level)	Automatic (for example, at 12.6 V) or manual
• End of charge thresholds with temperature compensation	For example, 14.1 V at 25°C and 13.83 V at 40°C

• Boost charge	allows for an occasional overcharge (after the disconnection of all loads)
• Electrical protection	against short-circuits (fuses or blocking diodes) and lightning
• Protection against reverse polarity	fuses or blocking diodes

(The voltage thresholds for 24 V systems are double those of 12 V systems.)

Other considerations:

- The discharge threshold determines approximately the maximum authorised discharge (or the **maximum depth of discharge DOD**), before the battery will be disconnected from the system and hence the loads. The higher the threshold, the longer the battery will last (for example, 11.9 V is better than 10.5 V).

- Temperature compensation: for most regulators, the end of charge threshold decreases automatically as temperature rises in order to preserve the life of the batteries (-0.018 to –0.030 V/°C).

  For example, if the threshold is 14.1 V at 25°C (manufacturer setting), but the regulator and the batteries are operating at an ambient temperature of 40°C, then the end of charge threshold will decrease automatically to: 14.1 – (0.018 x (40 – 25))= 13.83 V.

- The end of charge threshold on sealed batteries is always lower than that of vented batteries. Be careful when choosing a regulator to respect these thresholds.

Important: Read the technical notice of each regulator to know its specific characteristics (for example, the meaning of the signals and alarms, any internal electrical protections that may do away with the need for external fuses between the batteries and the regulator, etc.).

7. Batteries

Batteries are the weakest component of a PV system. As in a car, a battery may break down at any moment.

© JPL

It is possible to increase the lifespan of batteries, if they are properly sized, installed and maintained with care!

Principal characteristics:

Rated capacity (Ah)	For example, 100 Ah at C/100 and 20 °C
• Nominal voltage (V)	For example, 2 V, 6 V or 12 V
• Cycle life as a function of Daily Depth of Discharge (DDOD)	For example, 2 to 5 years (730 to 1825 cycles) according to the DDOD
• Electrolyte specific gravity / Open voltage Uoc / State of charge	For example, 1.24 at 20°C, open voltage of 12.5 V and a battery charged to 80 %
• Type of technology:	
Vented lead-acid	For example, car batteries or solar batteries regularly filled with distilled water
Sealed lead-acid	For example, maintenance free gel batteries
Nickel-manganese (Ni-mH) or Ion-lithium	For example, batteries for portable phones or lamp torches
• Self-discharge (%/month)	For example, 5 to 30 % for a car battery
• Voltage charge threshold / Voltage discharge threshold	For example, 14.5 / 11.4 V (refer to section 6)
• Charge current / Discharge current	For example, 5 A for a 100 Ah battery
• Energy efficiency (during charge and discharge)	For example, 70 % for car batteries
• Consumption of distilled water (litres/month)	For example, 1 litre every 3 months for a 100 Ah battery

Other considerations:

- In a solar system, the battery is successively charged and discharged on a daily basis (1 cycle per day). The battery **cycle life** refers to the number of cycles of charge / discharge a battery is able to support, without damage.

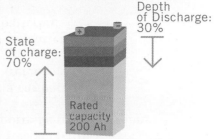

- The cycle life increases if the **daily depth of discharge** or DDOD, is a small percentage of the rated capacity of the battery (for example, for a car battery, if the DDOD is 50%, the cycle life can be 6 months or 182 cycles, but if the DDOD is 30%, the cycle life can be up to **2 years** or 730 cycles).

Cycle life as a function of DDOD and battery type

Type of plates	Car battery Thin plate	Vented 'Solar' Thick plate	Sealed (gel) Thick plate	Stationary vented Tubular
Unit capacity	(25 to 200 Ah)	(10 to 200 Ah)	(25 to 150 Ah)	(150 to 2000 Ah)
DDOD 10%	3 to 4 years	5 to 7 years	6 to 8 years	> 10 years
DDOD 20%	2 to 3 years	4 to 5 years	5 to 6 years	10 years
DDOD 30%	1.5 to 2 years	3 to 4 years	4 to 5 years	6 years
DDOD 50%	6 months to 1 year	1 to 2 years	2 to 3 years	4 years
DDOD 80%	2 months	3 to 6 months	1 to 2 years	2 years

(Source: manufacturer documentation, for a temperature of 25°C)

- Car batteries are less expensive. 'Solar' or stationary batteries are more expensive but can be more cost effective in the long run as they are better adapted and, if well used, will last longer (hence are less frequently replaced).

- Operating conditions greater than 25°C decrease the lifespan of all types of batteries, and that of sealed batteries even more so.

- Storage capacity depends on a number of factors. It decreases:

  - with a strong discharge current. Capacity is always indicated for a given intensity of discharge (for example, 75 Ah at C/100. If the discharge current is 75/100 = 0.75 A, the capacity of the battery will be 75 Ah but if the discharge current is greater, for example 7.5 A, the capacity will only be 60 Ah),
  - irreparably if the battery is left uncharged for several weeks,
  - with prolonged use at weak state of charge,
  - with poor usage habits and lack of regular maintenance (for example, low electrolyte levels), and
  - over time and at operating conditions greater than 25°C.

Variations in battery capacity as a function of temperature

Temperature	-10 °C	0 °C	10 °C	20 °C	25 °C	30 °C	40 °C
Correction factor to apply	0.72	0.83	0.91	0.98	1.00	1.02	1.05

For example, a 100 Ah C/100 battery at 25°C will have a capacity of 83 Ah at 0°C.

- The **state of charge** of a battery can be evaluated in 2 ways:

  - By measuring the density of the electrolyte within.
  - By measuring the **open circuit voltage** of the battery (Uoc).

Important: To measure the open circuit voltage, disconnect all electrical loads and PV array from the battery at least 30 minutes before taking the measurement.

© IPL

Measuring the open circuit voltage

The chart below provides examples of possible results (see also the diagram in **section 12.3**).

Open circuit voltage	>	State of charge	<	Electrolyte specific gravity
12.8 V	>	100%	<	1.28 g/l
12.5 V	>	70%	<	1.22 g/l
11.9 V	>	20%	<	1.12 g/l

- The size of the battery will depend on daily requirements, the length of time the system will operate without being recharged by the array, in the absence of sunlight (during which time the energy is furnished entirely by the battery) and the DDOD. Two examples of sizing are presented in **Annexes 1** and **2**.

  - An undersized battery will be less expensive at the outset, but will be exposed to deeper cycles of discharge and hence will have a shorter life.

  - An oversized battery will be more costly and will rarely be fully charged. It will then be prone to sulfatation, and as a consequence will have a shorter life as well.

Security issues

© JPL

- Do not allow metal objects or tools to link the negative and positive terminals of a battery.
- Be very careful when handling all batteries. Wear protective gloves and glasses.
- If a part of the body comes into contact with electrolyte, rinse it immediately and thoroughly with water. If electrolyte enters the eyes, rinse immediately with water and consult a doctor.
- Always wash your hands after handling a battery.
- Do not smoke or make sparks near batteries as there is a risk of explosion.

8. Loads and inverters

Loads are appliances such as lamps, radio-cassette players, televisions and refrigerators. Inverters and converters may also be necessary to adapt the input voltage for certain kinds of appliances.

With the aim of reducing the size and cost of systems, it is important to give preference to:

- appliances with the lowest power consumption for a given service,

- appliances that run directly on 12 or 24 V DC (to avoid the use of inverters), and

- positioning the appliances in such a way as to minimise the lengths of cable used while satisfying the client's wishes.

 Important: It is necessary to know the consumption of the appliances to be used. Such information is normally written on the appliance. If not, it is necessary to measure the power consumption (for example, measure the intensity with an ammeter and multiply the result by the input voltage. For television or radio cassette player, make this measurement with the volume set at maximum).

8.1. Lighting

Lighting must be chosen primarily for its capacity to provide a maximum amount of light for a minimum of power consumption (high efficiency lighting), and also for its longevity, cost and availability on the local market so as to ensure easy replacement.

In the majority of cases, fluorescent lights (compact bulbs or tubes) will be used. They provide the same lighting comfort and allow for the size of the system to be reduced by a factor of 3 or 4 when compared to incandescent bulbs.

Type of bulb	Standard incandescent	Low voltage halogen	Fluorescent	LED
Lighting efficiency (lumen/W)	5 to 10	15 to 30	40 to 70	20 to 30
Lighting quality	Good	Excellent	Good	Mediocre to good
Longevity (hours)	100 to 1 000	1 000 to 2 000	5 000	More than 5 000
Impact on the cost of the solar system (size of the battery and the panel)	Negative	Neutral	Excellent	Excellent
Examples of recommended use	3 to 10 W for short-term usage: toilets, hallways	5 to 20 W Reading corner and precise work	4 to 30 W All applications, reading corners, outside lighting	0.7 to 2 W Hallways, nightlights, external security lamps

 Important: Beware of information indicated on some bulbs or tubes. Certain lamps equipped with 8 W fluorescent tubes can consume up to 15 W, whereas others with 13 W tubes may consume only 9 W.

8.2. Televisions

Power consumption varies greatly depending on the brand and age of the appliance.
Televisions consume more power when they are AC, in colour, and as the size of the screen increases.

BLACK AND WHITE TV 14 INCHES (35 CM)		COLOUR TV 14 INCHES (35 CM)		COLOUR TV 17 INCHES (43 CM)	
12 V$_{DC}$		12 V$_{DC}$	230 V$_{AC}$	12 V$_{DC}$	230 V$_{AC}$
12 to 15 W		25 to 35 W	35 to 50 W	35 to 50 W	50 to 65 W

Important: Most radios, televisions and telephone chargers consume energy (between 2 and 15 W) when on stand-by, even if they are switched off! It is strongly recommended to install such appliances using an extension cord with an on/off switch or to unplug them when not in use.

8.3. Solar refrigerators

© JPL

Solar refrigerators are well insulated (7 to 15 cm of insulation) and of small capacity (50 to 150 litres internal volume), in order to reduce electrical consumption. They are not ordinary refrigerators.

Most are equipped with a 60 W compressor in 12 V DC (or 24 V DC). As an example, the compressor will operate for approximately 15 minutes per hour, about 25% of the time: 60 W x 24 h x 25% = 360 Wh/day.

Electrical consumption varies considerably according to the temperature at which the thermostat is set and the ambient temperature of the room where the refrigerator is located:

Influence of ambient temperature	25°C (Europe)	32°C (Cameroon)	43°C (Djibouti)
Refrigerator 150 litres (thermostat set at 4°C)	230 Wh/day	315 Wh/day	545 Wh/day
Freezer 150 litres (thermostat set at - 15°C)	450 Wh/day	615 Wh/day	1070 Wh/day

Assumptions: consumption calculated with a load of 2 kg of products per day and the door opened for 20 minutes per day.

Power consumption will more than double between the simple conservation of medicines/vaccines or foodstuff and the fabrication of ice. It will also increase if the door is kept open for long periods of time.

Rules to observe

- In order to size a solar system for a refrigerator, it is essential to know the conditions under which it will be used: the quantity and turnover of produce or products to be stored, the thermostat setting and the ambient temperature of the room.
- Installation: the refrigerator must be situated away from direct sunlight, in a well ventilated place that is as cool as possible. It is wise to install locks to control access to the unit.
- Maintenance: defrost the refrigerator with a warm cloth whenever the level of frost is greater than 5 mm. Never use metal objects to defrost the unit. Clean the back of the refrigerator regularly (the condenser).

Solar vaccine refrigerators must conform to standards set by the World Health Organisation.

8.4. Inverters DC/AC

An inverter is an apparatus capable of transforming direct current (DC) (also known as continuous current) into alternating current (AC).

Principal characteristics:

• **Nominal power (W)**	For example, 200 W (Nominal continuous output power at a temperature of 20°C).
• **Output voltage (V)**	For example, 230 V AC ± 5%, 50 Hz ± 5%. Bigger fluctuations may damage the electric appliances.
• **Input voltage (V)**	Between 10.5 V and 15 V. Beyond these limits, the inverter must be able to cut off its electric supply without being damaged.
• **Efficiency (%)**	For example, should be at least 75% in the range of 20 to 80% of the inverter's rated power.
• **Output signal**	For example, pure sinusoid, or quasi sinus.
• **Overcharge capacity (%)**	Capacity to furnish a power greater than its nominal power in order to absorb power/demand peaks when certain appliances are switched on (Televisions or electric motors). For example, 200% of nominal power for 10 seconds.
• **Standby consumption**	For example, 0.5 to 15 W
• **Electrical protection** (short circuit and overcharge)	Internal protection against short circuit on the AC output (with manual or automatic re-set) Protection against reverse polarity
• **Automatic detection of appliances**	Only found on high quality inverters. This reduces standby consumption greatly.

Comments valid for most inverters:

- The nominal power rating should be between 2 to 3 times greater than the power of the appliances it will supply (for example, choose a 200 W inverter for a 65 W television).
- Inverters (50 to 200 W) should be connected at the regulator level (refer to the diagram in **section 3.1**). Ensure that the regulator is capable of handling the current to be used by the AC appliances. If the inverter is equipped with a remote control, it must be installed directly to the battery. Exceptionally, an inverter without a remote control may be connected directly to the battery, but the battery will no longer be protected against deep discharges: inverters have a low voltage protection, but with a voltage threshold that is too low to protect the battery (for example, 10.5 V).
- An inverter is supplied with large incoming DC cables (at least 2.5 to 6 mm²) in order to reduce voltage drops. These must be connected to the regulator (or to the battery depending on the circumstances), without extending them!
- The use of an inverter renders a solar system more complex to design, install and use. Inverters are extremely difficult to repair, especially new generation models, composed essentially of high-technology electronic components.

It is imperative to choose only AC appliances that are very economical in terms of electricity consumption. This will reduce the size of the inverter, the PV modules and the batteries needed.

8.5. DC/DC Adapters

Adapters are used to reduce the voltage for appliances that function with lower voltage levels than 12 V DC. Most adapters provide the following voltages: 1.5 V; 3 V; 4.5 V; 6 V; 7.5 V; 9 V and 12 V. For example, an adapter must be set to 6 V for a radio that functions on 4 dry-cell batteries of 1.5 V each. Most dedicated 12 V adapters to recharge portable telephones have an output voltage between 3 and 4.5 V.

In addition to using fuses or circuit breakers, it is advisable to install a switch to turn off electricity supply from the inverter or the adapter. This saves the energy that is used in standby mode, even when no loads are in use.

9. Choice of cables and electrical protection equipment

Voltage drops occur primarily in **cables** and **fuses**. Cables should be sized so as to avoid voltage drops.

For cables in DC systems, voltage drops should not surpass the values noted here:

	12 V system	24 V system
Between PV module and regulator:	0.3 V maximum	0.6 V maximum
Between regulator and battery:	0.15 V maximum	0.3 V maximum
Between regulator and loads:	0.3 V maximum	0.6 V maximum

In practice:

• reduce cable lengths as much as possible,

• use big cables: such as 2 x 2.5 mm² minimum, and

• calculate voltage drops before installing or modifying an installation.

Voltage drop = Lc x R x I	**Lc**	Length of two-core cable
	I	Nominal intensity in the cable
	R	Electrical resistance of a two-core cable

Cable size in mm²	1	1.5	2.5	4	6	10	16
(R): Resistance (Ohm/metre)	0.04	0.0274	**0.01642**	0.01018	0.00678	0.0039	0.00248

For example, the voltage drop in a 15 m two-core cable (2 x 2.5 mm²) supplying an 8 W bulb (12 V – 0.6 A) is equal to 15 m x 0.01642 Ohm/m x 0.6 A= 0.15 V.

For systems supplied in kits: it is possible that the cross-section of the cables provided is less than 2.5 mm². Calculate whether the voltage drops will be acceptable or not.

Electrical protection

© S. Charmoy

Fuses or circuit breakers must be used to protect installations against short circuits or **overcharges** (see their placement on the diagram in **section 3.1**). In each case, fuses will be placed on the positive conductor.

The fuse rating should be slightly bigger than the maximum intensity to go through the cable (for example, 1.5 times the maximum current). Calculate the maximum intensity to go through the cable and choose the appropriate fuse (for example, 2, 3, 5, 10 or 16 A).

Certain regulators come equipped with fuses or other electrical protection devices against short circuits and overcharges. In this case, do not add more fuses as they will create additional voltage drops.

Protection against lightning and induced over-voltages may be necessary when the site is subject to frequent storms (for example, earthing, refer also to **section 11.4**).
When earthing is advised, all metal parts of the installation (for example, PV module frame, support structure) must be linked by a cable (yellow and green, minimum cross-section 10 mm²), then linked to a rod in the earth that should be in as humid a zone as possible.

Earthing techniques rely on security regulations concerning the protection of people and buildings. Refer to and respect national codes.

10. Quality control and procurement advice

It is critical to procure quality equipment at the best prices!

General advice for all equipment:
- Insist on obtaining all relevant **technical documentation**. The existence of clear documents including characteristics, instructions for installation, operation and maintenance is a sign of quality.
- Verify that the technical characteristics correspond to your sizing.
- Ask for **references** for the proposed components (for example, photographs of installations in the area, numbers of systems sold, etc.).
- Ask about **warranty conditions** and the possibility of **after sales services** (for example, replacement parts).

Advice for PV modules:
- Choose the module for its power rating in Wp, and not for its physical size. Two modules of the same technology, the same manufacturer and the same size may have very different power ratings (for example, 42 Wp or 52 Wp). If possible measure the Isc and compare it with a module that you know well.

- Give preference to modules that conform to the international manufacturing standards IEC-61215 for mono- or multi-crystalline modules and IEC 61646 for amorphous modules, or to the national norms used in your country.

  Manufacturing standards are guarantees of reliability and durability for PV modules.

- Give preference to modules with a serial number permanently engraved on the module and have this number noted on the invoice.

- Check where the module comes from, if it is new or used, in order to negotiate the price.
- Finally, compare modules by calculating the price per Wp (for example, €200 for a 50 Wp module = 4 €/Wp).

© IPL

Advice for regulators and batteries:

- For the regulator, choose a model with a temperature compensation feature if the system is to be used in ambient temperatures above 30°C or below 15°C (refer to **section 6**). Choose a model with indicators that are easily read by the users.
- If the supplier proposes smaller capacity batteries than you have calculated, ask for explanations as this will have an impact on the life of the batteries.
- Choose a single battery rather than two for a given capacity (one battery of 120 Ah – 12 V is preferable to two batteries of 60 Ah – 12 V giving longer life, less cabling and 6 cells instead of 12 to check electrolyte levels).
- Have the supplier carry out the initial charge of the battery. This has the double advantage of ensuring that the plates are formatted correctly and will help to validate the supplier's warranty. The inconvenience to this is that the battery must then be transported to the installation site without losing electrolyte and without delay.
- Buy electrolyte for putting the batteries into service and distilled water for maintenance from the battery supplier so as to ensure the quality of these products.
- For sealed batteries, measure the open circuit voltage. It should be greater than 12.6 V. If the battery has been stored for more than 6 months, from the fabrication date indicated on the battery, avoid buying it unless it has been recharged regularly.
- Finally, compare batteries of equal quality by calculating the price per Ah (for example, €70 for a battery of 100 Ah = 0.7 €/Ah).

© JPL

© JFL

Beware of fake regulators!
In this model there are no electrical
components for regulation at all

11. Installation of solar systems

The quality of the installation of a system will have a determining impact on the longevity of the system. A well-installed system will be your best publicity.

The recommended phases of installation are as follows:

PHASE 1	• Prepare and organise your work	As explained in **section 11.1**
PHASE 2	• Install the principal components (PV modules, regulator, battery) • Put the battery to charge	As explained in the installation procedures in **sections 11.2 to 11.4**
PHASE 3	• Install the appliances	As explained in **section 11.5**
PHASE 4	• Carry out the finishing touches (operational test and training the user)	As explained in **section 11.6**

11.1. Preparing and organising your work

Before installing the components, follow the steps below:

1. **Read all technical data and instructions** supplied with the equipment. Apply any recommendations concerning installation. Advice given in such guides should be adapted to the circumstances.

2. Ensure that **ALL tools and system components** are at the installation site, from the PV modules to the wood screws. Use the quotation form as a check list.

It is advisable to test the material to be installed before going to the site so as to avoid any unnecessary trips back to your base.

3. **LISTEN to the client and discuss with him or her** about where to place the different system components (appliances, regulator, etc.). Explain in simple terms the technical constraints of installation and find compromises to satisfy the client. Finalise the placement of each system component.

As a general rule, it is best to place the regulator and the battery near the centre of the house. This reduces cable lengths to lamps and electric outlets. The location should be well ventilated and safe for children.

4. Using chalk, mark horizontal and vertical lines on the walls to outline the placement of cables and system components. This will help during installation and ensure that the resulting work looks neat and proper.

5. Prepare rigid support structures (for example, wooden boards) for the regulators, lamps and switches if the walls are not sufficiently solid (for example, mud walls). Attach them solidly to the walls. It will then be easier to mount the system components.

Follow any national procedures or installation guides, where they exist.

© JPL

11.2. PV module installation procedure

1. Determine the exact placement of the module or array keeping in mind the following:

- no shade should fall on the array from neighbouring obstacles such as trees, walls, antennae, telephone poles or lines, etc.,
- limit the distance between the array and the battery,
- avoid dust deposits on the modules (as is common on roadside buildings),
- ensure easy and secure access to the array for cleaning and maintenance, and
- limit the possibility of theft or vandalism.

Most frequently, PV arrays are placed on rooftops of houses or buildings.

2. Design a sturdy support structure which will ensure that:

- The modules be **orientated** towards the south in the northern hemisphere (for example, Europe, Morocco, Mali, Laos, Sudan) and towards the north in the southern hemisphere (for example, Madagascar, French Polynesia, Zimbabwe).
- The modules be **inclined** to the following angles:
  a) for sites close to the equator where the latitude is between 0 and 10°: an angle of 10° to allow for rainwater to run off easily, and
  b) for sites where the latitude is greater than 10°, the modules will often be inclined to an angle equal to the latitude of the site in order to receive the maximum irradiation throughout the year, OR to an angle slightly greater (latitude + 10° or latitude + 20°) to receive the maximum irradiation during the least favourable months.
- The array must be installed at least 10 cm from the surface of the roof to allow for sufficient natural ventilation.

3. Install the support structure (use all precautions so as to avoid falls).

4. Check the voltage and the polarity inside the junction box on the solar panel.

---

* The north determined with a compass is the magnetic north. In theory, one should use the geographic north, but in most regions, the difference is not more that 15 degrees between the two, which does not have a great impact on the electricity production of PV modules.

5. Connect the cables ensuring that no water can penetrate the junction box (for example, pass the cables through a sealing gland, check the seal between the junction box and its cover).

6. Mount the PV modules on the support structure ensuring that the junction box is located at the highest point of the module.

7. Protect the cable from sunlight, unless it is a weatherproof and ultra-violet resistant cable.

8. Run the cable from the module to the regulator, **but do not yet connect it to the regulator**.

If the array is composed of several PV modules, it may be advisable to attach the modules to the support structure and to interconnect the modules before mounting the entire structure onto its final destination, the rooftop or a pole.

© JPL (pour toutes les images)

11.3. Battery installation procedure

This procedure applies to new vented batteries that have not yet been filled with electrolyte. The electrolyte should be supplied separately in a plastic container.

© Systèmes Solaires

Important

When preparing a battery, it is important to work in a clean and well-ventilated place.

1. Measure the open voltage of the battery. It should be zero.

2. Measure the specific gravity of the electrolyte supplied in the container. It should be the same as indicated on the battery documentation (for example, 1.24 to 1.28).

3. Clean the top cover of the battery with a dry clean cloth.

4. Remove the caps.

5. Fill the battery with electrolyte, cell by cell, using a funnel, up to the minimum level indicated on the battery. Let the battery settle for 20 minutes (the battery will heat up a bit).

6. Measure the voltage. It should be greater than 12 V.

7. Top up the level of electrolyte to the maximum level in each cell.

8. Replace the caps and clean the top of the battery with a clean dry cloth.

9. Do not install the battery directly on the floor, but in a battery box or on a wooden stand.

10. Strip the ends of the cables in order to connect them to the battery clamps, but **do not connect the clamps to the + and – terminals at this stage**.

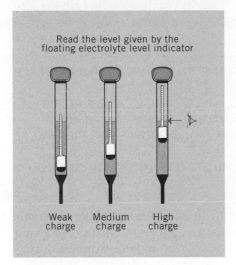

Read the level given by the
floating electrolyte level indicator

| Weak charge | Medium charge | High charge |

The ideal battery box will have the following characteristics:

- made of plastic so as to contain any leaks or spills of electrolyte,
- large enough to store a bottle of distilled water within it,
- designed with ventilation holes,
- designed such that the level of electrolyte can be checked without taking the battery from the box,
- can be locked with a key or padlock, and
- the cover is fitted at an angle so as to avoid people using the box as a stool or a shelf.

In the absence of plastic boxes, hardwood boxes can be built locally to meet these specifications.

In public buildings, batteries should only be accessible to authorised personnel.

The diagram on the left shows the correct position to read the hydrometer. The position of the floater depends on the state of charge of the battery.

11.4. Regulator installation procedure – charging the battery

1. Install the regulator where the user will have easy access, this will often be in the same room as the battery. The user's notice should be placed next to the regulator (see an example of a user's notice in **Annex 6**).

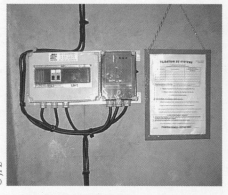

2. Check that the regulator is set to the type of battery used in the system, either 'vented' or 'sealed'. This often means setting a small switch on the regulator (refer to the technical specifications of the regulator).

3. Install the regulator at a height of 1.5 m (eye level), ideally on a wooden support structure and aligned directly over the battery.

4. Connect the cables to the regulator in the order directed by the manufacturer (usually in the following sequence: 1) regulator to the battery, 2) module to the regulator). Then insert a fuse between the battery and the regulator.

5. Grease the battery terminals and clamps with petroleum jelly (Vaseline).

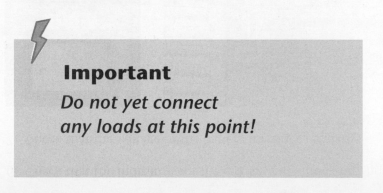

Important

Do not yet connect any loads at this point!

At this point in the installation, the module will begin to charge the battery. This will allow one to check that the battery is charging well while proceeding with the rest of the work (installation of the cables, switches, sockets and the training of the users).

6. Check that the indicators on the regulator are indicating normal functioning of the system.

7. Check that the voltage of the battery increases regularly.

Regulator installed on a wooden support panel

Regulator with cables in ducts

For sites known to have frequent and dangerous storms, it is possible to protect small systems by installing a bipolar switch near the regulator that will isolate the module cable from the rest of the installation. In such cases it is imperative to train the client to turn off the switch before a storm and to turn it on again after the storm.

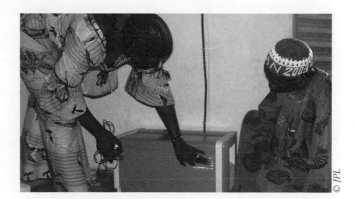

Some manufacturers propose a battery box with an integrated regulator as part of a kit

11.5. Loads installation and cabling procedure

'HINTS' for lamps:

- Install lamps as close to the lighting need as possible (for example, centred above a table in a dining room or at the head of a bed for reading).

- Do not install lamps higher than 2.5 m. If necessary, use chains or a wooden support structure to lower the lamp to this level.

- Advise the client to paint the walls and ceiling white, or at least the area surrounding the lamp, for a better diffusion of the light.

- For lamps fitted outside, install a shield to protect the lamp from the rain (for example, use a piece of corrugated iron roof).

'HINTS' for electric sockets:

© JPL

- Install sockets at least 20 cm from the floor.
- Install them firmly to avoid loosening over time.
- Connect the 3 pins DC female sockets in the following manner: connect the positive cable to the two poles 'Phase' and 'Neutral' (make a bridge inside the female socket), and the negative cable to the pole 'Earth'. This will avoid short circuits in the case of an AC appliance being plugged in.

'HINTS' for switches:

- Install switches firmly at 1.2 m from the ground, just on the inside of the room to be lit and on the side of the door with the door handle.
- Write the positions I (on) and O (off) with a permanent marker, if it is not clearly visible on the switch.

'HINTS' for cabling:

- Respect cable lengths and cross-sections as defined in the initial sizing and quotation forms.
- Always run cables horizontally and vertically, never diagonally up a wall.
- Attach cable clips to the wall at 25 to 30 cm intervals.
- Do not leave any slack in the cables as they can be damaged easily.
- Ensure that the cables are straight but not pulled too tightly.
- Leave extra cable lengths near the battery, the regulator and the modules (for example, about 20 cm). This will facilitate maintenance and any eventual replacement work to be carried out.
- Respect colour codes (for example, red for positive, black for negative).
- Double check polarity at regular intervals.
- Make all the connections between the cables inside junction boxes and using connector blocks. Avoid using spliced or twisted joints at any price.
- Always use cables that are at least 2.5 mm² except for those loads that consume less than 5 W (for example, LED lamps) – calculate the voltage drops.
- Do not use any existing cabling, unless you have verified if the length and cross-section respects what is quoted on the sizing form.

Always install switches and electric sockets in the same way (same height and position) so that the electrical installation looks neat and well planned.

11.6. Finishing touches on the installation

1. Measure the open circuit voltage of the battery to control that it has been recharged since step **11.4**.

2. Connect the cables from the loads to the regulator and insert or close any fuses of the load circuit.

3. Turn on each of the loads and ensure that each is functioning properly.

4. Check that the indicators on the regulator are functioning normally and measure the voltage at the terminals of the regulator (module, battery and loads).

The system is functioning. That's good, but the installation is not completed! Continue your work!

5. Using a permanent marker, indicate the date the system has been put into service on all the components: the regulator, the battery and the loads. Leave your contact information on the battery box as well as instructions explaining 'Electric Danger / Explosive / No Smoking'.

6. Take note of all relevant information pertaining to the components so as to facilitate any eventual replacement needs (serial numbers, relevant voltage drops between the regulator and the loads). This information along with the initial sizing information will constitute the identity card of the system.

7. Create a logbook for the system to be left with the owner. It will be used to record all interventions by the users and the technician such as adding distilled water to the battery, replacing any bulbs and routine maintenance and servicing information.

8. A user's notice should be posted near the regulator. This poster should provide information about how and when to carry out regular maintenance (see an example in **Annex 6**).

9. **Train the user:**
   - about using the system: *inform the user about how long appliances can be used, which types of appliances can be used and which must be avoided at all cost.*

   - about regular maintenance: *after explaining the procedures,* **make the user do the tasks him or herself.** *For example, putting up a ladder to reach the panels and then cleaning the panels safely, checking the electrolyte level and then adding distilled water to the battery.*

   - about small repairs: *such as changing a fluorescent tube...or simply waiting a few days for the battery to be fully recharged!*

© S. Charmoy

10. Leave your contact information or that of the person to call for repairs. One day the system may breakdown, and the client will need the intervention of a good technician.

Two further important points:

Explain to the user that it is better to wait five days before fully using the system. This will help to prolong the life of the battery.

Supply a bottle of distilled water to be kept in the battery box.

12. Maintenance and servicing of small solar systems

Solar systems require minimal but essential maintenance and servicing.

There are two levels of maintenance:

- The first concerns **routine maintenance** that must be carried out regularly by the user. This involves the straightforward tasks of cleaning the PV array and removing any obstacles that create shade, checking the level of electrolyte in the battery and adding distilled water if necessary, and finally replacing any bulbs as necessary. The technician must be assured that these tasks are feasible for the user and carried out correctly and regularly.

- The second level is **servicing** that must be carried out by the technician who is equipped with the necessary skills and tools for the work. During servicing, all the principal components of the system will be checked, according to procedures explained in this chapter. Servicing should be carried out every six months.

Routine maintenance and servicing are preventive measures (to be carried out regularly when the system is operating well) to ensure the continuity of electricity supply.

Suggested servicing sequence:

PHASE 1 •	Prepare your work (with your toolbox at hand)	As explained in **section 12.1**
PHASE 2 •	Inspect the PV modules, regulator, battery, etc.	As explained in **sections 12.2** to **12.5**
PHASE 3 •	Proceed to the finishing touches (e.g.: training the user)	As explained in **section 12.6**

12.1. Preparing your work

1. **DISCUSS with the user**, before beginning your work. The user is your principal source of information about the health of the system. Enquire about which aspects of the system are satisfactory and which pose any problems. The answers to such questions will help you to do a better job.

2. **Consult the logbook** of the system and any notes you may have taken.

Regulator tampered with by a user

3. Check whether any **new loads have been added**, as compared to what the system was originally designed for.

4. Check that no components have been **tampered with or damaged**.

5. **Clean each component** with the help of the user. This will give you an idea of how she or he takes care of the system when you are not there.

Important

- *Follow systematically step by step the procedures explained here for each component.*

- *Follow any specific instructions or procedures found in the maintenance manual(s) provided by the manufacturers, whenever they are available.*

12.2. PV module servicing procedure

1. Clean the array with water, either early in the morning or late in the evening (do not use any soaps or detergents).

2. Check that the array is still mounted, orientated and inclined correctly.

3. Check the modules for discoloured or broken cells or any corrosion between cells.

4. Check that there is no shade on the modules (for example, a recently constructed building, a tree that has grown, a TV antenna).

5. Check that there are no bird or insect nests installed behind the array. If there are, remove them.

Checking if the bolts are still tight on the support structure of a PV array.

These trees must be trimmed back.

6. Check that the junction box is watertight.

7. For a PV array that has been earthed, check the continuity of the earthing from the array to the buried earth rod.

8.

Important

If you suspect that the array does not charge the battery well, follow the special step number 8 described on the following page, otherwise proceed to step 9.

9. Tighten all connections.

10. Measure the voltages of the array and the battery at the level of the regulator. During the day, the array voltage should be slightly higher than the battery voltage when all the loads are switched on (from 0.2 to 1 V).

Maintenance in 2005 of a module installed in 1988 in the Democratic Republic of the Congo: still functioning well!

© S. Charnoy

Special procedure 8 (if you suspect that the array is not charging the battery well)

8.1 Disconnect the array from the regulator (as a precaution, cover the array with a sheet or leaves).

8.2 *Comparison test of voltage Uoc*: measure the open circuit voltage of the PV array to be tested. Immediately after, carry out the same measurement on a neighbouring module or a reference module (for example a 5 Wp module). Ensure that the second module is clean and positioned exactly as the array being checked. Record the values in a table similar to the example below: *Example of Uoc and Isc tests.*

Typical values of Uoc and Isc, measured at noon

Power of the module	5 Wp	20 Wp	30 Wp	40 Wp	50 Wp	60 Wp	70 Wp	80 Wp
Isc (A)	0.30	1.2	1.80	2.4	3.0	3.60	4.20	4.8
Uco (V)	19 to 22 V whatever the power rating for modules composed of 36 cells							

8.3 *Comparison test of current Isc*: Measure the Isc of the array and, immediately after, measure the Isc of the reference module following the same procedure (same orientation, same inclination). Record the values in the table below.

8.4 Calculate the verification ratios of the Isc and Uoc values, both measured and theoretical, as in the following example (the theoretical values of Isc et Uoc are provided by the manufacturer and written on the label of the modules). If the measured ratio of Uoc and Isc are within 20% of the theoretical ratios, then the array is functioning correctly.

8.5 If this is not the case, disconnect the modules from the array and repeat the comparison tests for each module individually so as to determine which module is defective. In the case of a defective module, refer to **section 13.1**.

8.6 **Return to step 9 (section 12.2)**

Example of Uoc and Isc tests:

	Weather conditions: sunny				Time of test: 11:30				Date: 10 May 2008	
	Test array				Reference array or module				Comparison	
	Peak power (Wp)	No. of Modules	Isc	Uoc	Peak power (Wp)	No. of Modules	Isc	Uoc	Ratio Isc	Ratio Uoc
Theoretical Values	110	2	7	21.7	10	1	0.64	21.2	7/0.64=10.9	21.7/21.2=1.02
Measured Values	-	-	5	18	-	-	0.44	16	5/0.44=11.3	18/16= 1.12
									11.3/10.9=1.04	1.12/1.02=1.1
									<1.2 Ok!	<1.2 Ok!

Uoc and Isc tests must be carried out at high levels of irradiance (neither in the rain, nor in the early morning or late evening).

If the array is composed of modules in parallel, add the theoretical values of Isc for each module to know the value of the theoretical value of Isc for the array. (for example, 3.5 x 2 = 7). The Uoc value of the array is equal to that of one of the modules.

12.3. Battery maintenance procedure

1. Always begin by asking the user:
   - if she or he has distilled water in stock, and if so how much?
   - if distilled water has been added to the battery, if so how much and in which cells?
   - if the level of electrolyte is above the plates?
   - where the distilled water comes from?
   - in which container has it been stored?
   - if she or he thinks that the battery is 'tired', and why?

2. Remove the battery from any charge (for example, disconnect the cable from the PV array at the level of the regulator) and switch off all the loads. Wait 30 minutes before taking any measurements.

    It is advisable to wear protective gloves and glasses while servicing the battery and to have a basin of water nearby in order to wash any eventual splashes of electrolyte.

3. Use this time to perform a visual inspection to detect any leaks in the battery container. Clean and dry the battery top.

4. Remove the battery caps and check for any dirt or foreign particles that may have fallen into the cells. If there are any, try to remove them using a non-metal tool.

5. Measure and record the open voltage.

6. Measure the specific gravity and temperature of the electrolyte:
   - In each cell, pump once, replace the electrolyte back in the same cell, pump a second time and read the specific gravity (record the value, for example: 1.150; 1.260 …).
   - Put the electrolyte back into the cell from which it came (do not mix electrolyte from different cells).

Adding distilled water

7. If the battery is functioning well (check this against the manufacturer's data), reconnect it to the PV array. The voltage should be greater than that recorded in Step 5. If there are any problems with the battery, refer to **section 13.3**.

8. Check the level of electrolyte.

9. If necessary, add distilled water using a plastic funnel (be careful not to touch the plates with the funnel, this can damage them). NEVER fill a battery with electrolyte if it is discharged. Always recharge the battery first.

Adding distilled water

10. Replace each cap ensuring that its ventilation hole is not obstructed.

11. Clean the terminals with sand paper or a wire brush if necessary.

12. Cover the terminals and clamps with petroleum jelly (Vaseline) in order to avoid corrosion and reconnect the cables.

13. Measure the voltage under a standard load charge and then leave the battery to recharge fully.

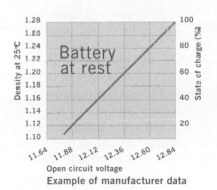

Example of manufacturer data

About step 13, it is useful to measure the voltage drop of the battery when a standard load is connected (for example, a 50 W appliance for a 100 Ah battery). If this information is recorded in the logbook when the battery is new and then periodically thereafter, then it will be possible to detect any losses in battery capacity. (The value of the voltage drop will increase over time until it reaches an unacceptable level. It will then be possible to change the battery before complete failure occurs.)

12.4. Regulator servicing procedure

1. Clean the outside of the regulator box with a clean, dry cloth. Dust and insect nests can prevent the regulator from cooling properly.

2. Ensure that the box is well mounted on the wall.

3. Take off the cover (this may be impossible for some types of regulator).

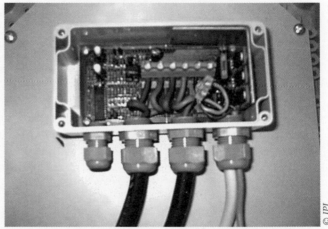

4. Check that no component, cable or fuse is giving off excessive heat. Check that no cables have been added. Inspect and tighten each connection.

5. Check that the indicators and dials (for example, LEDs or voltmeters) are providing coherent information (especially concerning the battery voltage).

6. Check that the cut-off and reconnection thresholds conform to those indicated by the manufacturer.

7. Check that the end of charge voltage threshold conform to those indicated by the regulator manufacturer.

8. Switch on some of the loads. Then at the regulator level, compare the voltage of the array to the voltage of the battery being charged. The array voltage should be greater than the battery voltage (from 0.1 to 1 V maximum).

Hint for servicing: always have a low capacity sealed battery at hand (for example, 7 Ah - 12 V). Connect this battery in the place of the client's battery and carry out the following tests: discharge threshold and end of charge threshold.
Another idea is to have a stabilized power supply which allows you to artificially vary the voltage entering the regulator (this is ideal).

It is best to perform the servicing procedures when it is sunny and around two o'clock in the afternoon (14:00 hours). At this point the battery will be almost fully charged. Measure the voltage at the battery terminals. This measurement should be comparable to the value on the technical notice keeping in mind the compensation for temperature.

9. At the regulator level, compare the voltage of the battery with the voltage of the loads circuit, with at least one of the loads switched on. The battery voltage should be greater than the voltage of the loads circuit (from 0.1 to 0.5 V).

10. Double-check and tighten the connections one last time.

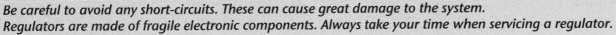

Important

Be careful to avoid any short-circuits. These can cause great damage to the system.
Regulators are made of fragile electronic components. Always take your time when servicing a regulator.

12.5. Loads and cabling servicing procedure

Recommendations for loads

Each type of load or appliance has its specific servicing requirements and it is not possible to cover specifically each type here. However there are some general recommendations to follow:

- Check whether any new loads have been connected to the system, apart from those initially planned.

- Clean and dust the different appliances (for example, the lamps) with the client and tighten all cabling connections.

- Measure the power consumption of the appliances if the client is complaining that the battery is always discharged. Any risk of over-consumption will shorten the life of the battery. Using a multimeter, measure the current consumed by each appliance and its input voltage, then calculate the power consumption (P = U x I). Compare this to the power indicated on the appliance itself.

- Measure voltage drops in the cables.

- Replace any blackened fluorescent tubes, only at the request of the client. After its replacement, calculate its lifetime. It should normally be between 3,000 and 5,000 hours (a tube that stops working after 3 years having functioned 4 hours per day will have functioned for a total of 3 x 365 days x 4 hours = 4,380 hours). If the tube has blackened prematurely, check the input voltage of the lamp while it is switched on as it is probably too low (for example, 11 V). In this case, reduce the cable resistance by using a thicker cable (or a cable of larger cross sectional area).

- For solar refrigerators, measure the current drawn and the length of the on/off cycles over a period of several hours. This will allow you to calculate the daily consumption (refer to **section 8.3**). Measure the operating temperature and finally, defrost the refrigerator if necessary.

- Check for and remove any stand-by power consumption (found on DC/DC converters, DC/AC inverters, televisions) by installing an on/off switch.

- Check all fuses and ensure that they have not been tampered with (for example, replaced by copper wires). In such cases, remove the copper wire and install a fuse.

- For inverters, measure the AC output voltage.

Recommendations for cabling

- Ensure that all cables are firmly attached and do not hesitate to remove any slack in the cables. Do not wait until a cable becomes so loose that one can hang something from it. Such cables encourage untidiness and children can pull on them.

- Ensure that no stripped wires are in evidence (or hidden elsewhere). These will be liable to unwanted or rogue connections.

Replace this connection with a connector block

Carrying out servicing means tightening loose fittings as well

12.6. Finishing touches for servicing

1. Using a permanent marker, indicate the installation date on any replacement parts installed.

2. Record all measurements and test results in the system logbook for future reference.

3. Invite the client to examine the system with you, making sure that each load is functioning correctly.

4. Explain the actions carried out during the servicing and show the client any parts that may have been replaced.

5. **Take the time to train the user:**
   - about using the system: *explain the length of time each appliance can be used and what must be avoided at all costs.*

   - about routine maintenance that she or he must do regularly: ***Make the client do the tasks him or herself*** *rather than simply showing what needs to be done. For example, cleaning the modules, checking the electrolyte level in the batteries and adding distilled water when necessary.*

   - about small breakdowns: *changing a fluorescent bulb...or simply waiting a few days for the battery to recharge!*

© IPL

6. Suggest to the client that, for the seven days following maintenance, he or she should use the system only minimally. This will ensure that the battery is fully recharged.

7. Leave your contact information, or that of another qualified technician, with the client. One day there will be a breakdown and the client or the user will need to get in touch with you.

Stage 1: I write the replacement date on the battery cover and also on the lamp

13. Recurrent problems and solutions

Solutions to recurrent problems are proposed in this chapter. However, they will only be of use if you are able to adopt the spirit of a 'problem-solver,' that is to say, remain calm, concentrated, conscientious, humble and honest... and well-equipped (tools and documents).

Try to adopt the following simple but reliable method:

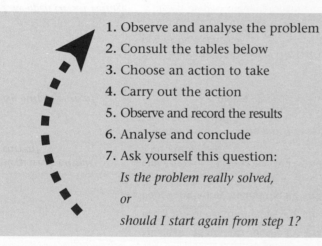

1. Observe and analyse the problem
2. Consult the tables below
3. Choose an action to take
4. Carry out the action
5. Observe and record the results
6. Analyse and conclude
7. Ask yourself this question:
   Is the problem really solved,
   or
   should I start again from step 1?

© S. Charmoy

Even when the faulty component is not the battery itself, most other faults will lead to its premature and definitive failure. It is therefore absolutely necessary to repair any faults as soon as possible.

13.1. Solar panel

Problem	Causes	Solutions
Weak output current	Too much dust	Clean the array. Modify the implantation if cleaning is not possible
	Shade on all or a part of the PV array	Remove the source of the shade
	Badly orientated or inclined PV array	Modify the orientation or inclination
	Poor ventilation around the PV array	Clean behind the array and modify the implantation if necessary
Very weak output current	One (or more) cells is covered by a leaf or a bird dropping	Clean and/or cut the obstructing branches
No output current	The connections in the junction box are loose or corroded	Clean and tighten. Drill a small hole (1 mm) at the bottom of the junction box to allow condensation to evacuate
	By-pass diode blown (short circuit)	Change the by-pass diode or simply remove it if no replacements are available (in the case of 12 or 24 V systems)
	Severed connection inside the junction box or between cells	If possible, scrape open the area behind the module and attempt to repair the connection by welding. Repair the module with silicone to ensure water tightness
Low open circuit voltage (less than 12 V at noon)	A blown by-pass diode (probably from lightning)	Change the by-pass diode or simply remove it if no replacements are available
Broken glass on a module	Vandalism	The module can still work for years, until the point where humidity corrodes the connections between cells. Change the module, if the Isc and Uoc are incorrect.
	Module struck directly by lightning	
	Fabrication defect	Check that the support structure does not provoke any mechanical constraints on the modules.
		Contact the supplier if the module is still under warranty

13.2. Regulator

Problem	Causes	Solutions
Unusual heat emitted from regulator body	The cable connections arriving in the regulator are loose	Tighten all connections (some heat dissipation is normal for some regulators)
No appliance is functioning	Battery discharged	Check the voltage of the battery
	Blown fuses at the level of the regulator, battery circuit or loads	Change the fuse(s)
Incorrect threshold voltages	Faulty components Regulator has been tampered with	Adjust the regulation thresholds or replace the regulator before this problem causes the battery to deteriorate
Regulator short-circuited or shunted	Usually done by the user to get more power from the battery	Remove the shunt and explain to the user the function of the regulator
Indicators giving false information	Many possible reasons	Adjust or replace the indicators (or the regulator itself)
Regulator cuts the loads too early	Damaged regulator or Battery in its final stages of life (sulphated battery)	Check the regulator thresholds. If they are normal, the battery is probably sulphated (**section 13.3: Solution 'S'**)
Regulator cuts the loads but the battery appears fully charged	The loads are drawing too high a current, inducing too great a voltage drop, leading to regulator cut-off	Replace the battery with one of greater capacity (this will reduce the voltage drop)
	Battery sulphated or damaged	See **section 13.3: Solution 'S'**

Example of correct regulator thresholds
(case of an all or nothing regulator)

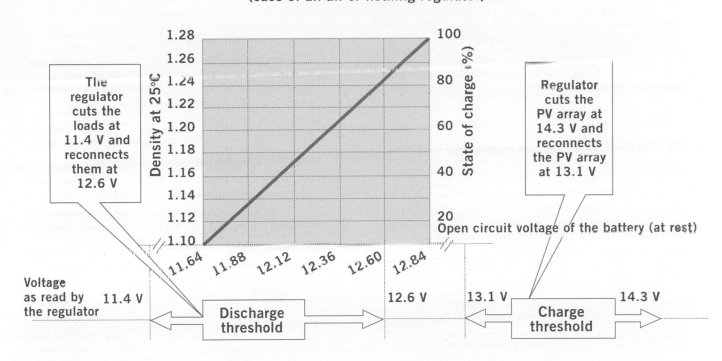

The regulator cuts the loads at 11.4 V and reconnects them at 12.6 V

Regulator cuts the PV array at 14.3 V and reconnects the PV array at 13.1 V

Density at 25°C

State of charge (%)

Open circuit voltage of the battery (at rest)

11.64 11.88 12.12 12.36 12.60 12.84

Voltage as read by the regulator

11.4 V

Discharge threshold

12.6 V

13.1 V

Charge threshold

14.3 V

13.3. Battery

Most breakdowns result from the battery losing its capacity. This is primarily caused by the number and depth of the cycles to which the battery has been subjected, and if it has functioned during extreme states of charge (such as overcharge, undercharge or deep discharge).

Important
The solutions to problems may depend on the type of battery, vented or sealed. The tables below mention these specific cases.

Vented and sealed 12 V batteries

Problem	Causes	Solutions
Permanent low state of charge and battery capacity reduced prematurely	Inadequate power supply for the required needs (number of modules insufficient, faulty regulator) or overuse.	Resize the PV system to meet needs before the batteries become sulphated
Battery heats up during charging, lots of bubbling and gassing	Charging current is too high	Reduce the charging current (check the sizing)
	End of charge threshold set too high	Check the regulator
High self-discharge	Presence of conductive deposits and / or humidity on the battery	Clean and dry the top of the battery. The battery must be stored in a cool and well-ventilated place
	Poor ventilation where the battery is stored	
	Battery in the last stages of life (corrosion of the plates)	Replace the battery

Problem	Causes	Solutions
Open circuit tension less than 9 V	Most likely a damaged battery	Replace the battery
Strong odour in the room or the battery box	Insufficient ventilation	Make ventilation holes on the top and bottom of the battery box
Batteries in parallel prematurely damaged	Batteries of different capacity, age or manufacturer connected in parallel	Never put more than 3 batteries in parallel Replace batteries in parallel with a single large battery
	Difference in cable lengths for putting batteries in parallel (one battery is better charged than another)	The cable lengths must be strictly identical and sufficiently large (minimum 4 mm²)
Corroded battery terminals	Spilled electrolyte from the cells – lack of maintenance	Clean the battery with a dry cloth, grease the terminals and clamps with petroleum jelly and reconnect the cables
Open circuit voltage around 10.5 V when the battery is charged and the battery still has a good capacity	One of the cells is destroyed and in short circuit	Replace the battery (or attempt to have the cell replaced if the battery has been in service for less than 6 months)

Vented and sealed 12 V batteries

Problem	Causes	Solutions
Voltage increases very fast whenever the regulator connects the PV array	Loose connections create resistances that affect the voltage readings by the regulator.	Clean and tighten the connections.
'the battery refuses to charge'	The battery is sulphated. Phenomenon appearing in old batteries and those left in a state of under-charge for several weeks. Such a battery has a strong internal resistance and when a current is applied, its voltage rises rapidly to cross the end of charge threshold of the regulator, whereas only a small amount of current has been stored.	**Solution 'S':** 'Soft' recharge of the battery for 7 days, to ensure that the battery receives a sufficient number of Ah (1.3 to 1.5 times its capacity) to be carried out in the following conditions: *For vented batteries*: Charge the battery **without** the regulator. The voltage will be greater than 15 V at the end of charge If this charge fails, attempt a curative treatment (see box 13.3.1). If this fails, replace the battery. *For sealed batteries*: Charge the battery **with** the regulator. The voltage must not surpass the end of charge threshold of the regulator (14.1 V). If this fails, replace the battery.
Voltage drops quickly as soon as the loads are switched on. The regulator cuts off the loads	The battery is sulphated. The internal resistance of the battery makes the voltage drop, the regulator cuts off the loads.	**Refer to solution 'S'.**
	Loads consume too much current for the capacity of the battery (for example, 10 A on a 40 Ah battery).	Modify the installation (for example, increase the capacity of the battery).
	Battery is discharged.	Recharge the battery.

Vented 12 V batteries

Problem	Causes	Solutions
Specific gravity of the electrolyte less than 1.24 even after a full recharge	The battery is sulphated.	**Refer to solution 'S'.**
Specific gravity of the electrolyte less than 1.100	The battery (or at least one of the cells) is most likely damaged. The battery is very old.	**Refer to solution 'S'.**
Distilled water consumption varies greatly between cells	Battery approaching the end of its life: cells sulphated. The cell with the lowest level is that which is sulphated.	**Refer to solution 'S'.**
Low specific gravity of the electrolyte and low voltage	Battery has been insufficiently charged for several days or weeks. Stratification of the electrolyte (the specific gravity at the bottom of the cell is lower than at the top of the cell).	Charge the battery with the array for at least 10 days with all loads cut off (using an end of charge threshold of 14.7 V), OR have the battery charged in a city centre with mains electricity for 3 days (using an end of charge threshold of 14.7 V). You should see gas bubbles being emitted from the top of the battery.
High consumption of distilled water in all the cells	Room where the battery is stored is too warm.	Improve ventilation and cooling of the room.
	End of charge threshold too high.	Lower the end of charge threshold.
	Charge current too high.	Check the sizing of the system.
	Deep discharge cycles too frequent or battery at the end of its life	Change the battery.
Insufficient level of electrolyte	Lack of maintenance.	Top up the level of electrolyte to maximum.
Plates in contact with the air	Lack of maintenance (lack of electrolyte).	Replace the battery (the plates are most likely irreversibly damaged).
Electrolyte has an unusual odour	Foreign particles in the battery cells.	Remove the foreign particles.
	Low quality distilled water.	Check the quality of the distilled water.

13.3.1. Hints for restoring a sulphated vented battery

Important
Use this method after careful diagnosis of the problem and after having tried solution 'S' described above.

Every technician has his or her own techniques for extending the life of a battery once it has been sulphated. These can help to recuperate a part of the original capacity of the battery and prolong its life for a few weeks or months.

Here is one such technique, step by step:

1. Drain the electrolyte from the battery (do not drain electrolyte onto the ground).
2. Refill the battery with distilled water.
3. Charge the battery with a charge current that is about 10% of the capacity of the battery (for example, 10 A for a 100 Ah battery) for 24 hours.
4. Measure the specific gravity: if it is about 1.150, repeat the operation (drain the battery and fill again with distilled water and recharge).
5. Measure the specific gravity: if it is between 1.050 and 1.100, drain the battery.
6. Fill with electrolyte (1.24 or 1.28 according to the type of battery). Do not reuse the old electrolyte.
7. Recharge the battery for 15 hours (with a charge current that is 10% of the capacity of the battery).
8. Measure the capacity of the battery (with a discharge current corresponding to the loads used by the client).

This method implies the purchase of several litres of distilled water and electrolyte. Its cost is not negligible. In many cases it is more cost effective to install a new battery.

Remark
It is impossible to carry out this procedure on sealed batteries.

13.4. Breakdowns on loads and cabling

Problem	Causes	Solutions
Appliance is not working correctly	Loose connection or cables cut. Cables eaten by rodents. Inversed polarities.	Check all the connections and polarities.
	Voltages drops too severe.	Tighten connections. Check the size of the cables.
	Internal problem of the appliance.	Repair or replace.
Premature blackening of fluorescent tubes	Voltage supplied to lamps is too low (9 to 10 V) or too high (15 V).	Check the voltage drops in the distribution circuits. Check the charge and discharge thresholds on the regulator.
Fluorescent tube does not light up	Blown tube or ballast.	Measure the continuity of electrodes at each end of the tube. If there is no continuity, change the tube. If there is continuity, take apart the lamp and look for the blown parts to repair or change.
Blown fuse or circuit breaker 'off'	Insufficient fuse or circuit breaker rating or appliance too powerful. Short circuit in a cable.	Calculate the maximum current when all the loads are switched on. Choose a slightly larger rated fuse.
Cables too small	Installation tampered with by user. Rogue extension to the installation.	Modify the cabling accordingly.
Inverter 'low voltage' default	Battery discharged or the cables from battery to inverter are not big enough.	Reduce significantly the use of loads and wait for the battery to be recharged – change the cables.
Inverter 'temperature' default	Poor ventilation (or a broken cooling fan). Inverter in overcharge.	Ensure good ventilation (dust-free and well-positioned), Check the sizing of the inverter.
Batteries discharged on a refrigerator installation	Refrigerator overloaded with goods. No defrosting, Door opened too frequently	Train the user.
	System installed in a room that is too warm. Poor seal on the refrigerator door. Insufficient ventilation behind the condenser.	Modify the installation. Check the current consumed by the compressor and the length of the on/off cycles.
	Thermostat not well adjusted (too cold).	Adjust the thermostat.
	Leak of refrigerant gas.	Call in a refrigeration technician.
Solar refrigerator does not produce cold	Leak of refrigerant gas. Thermostat not adjusted properly, etc. Damaged electronic card.	Call in a refrigeration technician. Take care to monitor energy consumption after reparation.

14. List of necessary tools

The essentials: a toolbox or bag should contain:

• Compass	• Set of screwdrivers (2 flathead and 2 Philips)
• Multimeter (measures continuous current up to 10 A)	• Adjustable pliers
• Hydrometer	• Adjustable wrench
• Spirit level	• Knife
• Tape measure (2 to 3 m)	• Hammer
• Permanent marker	• Plastic funnel
• Calculator (solar!)	• Filter for electrolyte (for example, nylon stocking)
• Notebooks, pencils, pencil sharpener and rubber	• Insulation tape
• Technical documentation about PV products, blank sizing and quotation forms and of course, this book!	• Cloths or rags (for cleaning)
	• Chalk

Useful, but not indispensable:

• Angle finder	• Cable cutter
• Chisel	• Cable stripper
• Hand drill and bits	• Square
• Welding iron 30 W - 12 V	• Small crystalline module (5 to 10 Wp)

Practical, but not always necessary:

• Carpentry tools (jack plane)

• Ladder (the client must provide one for cleaning the array)

• Plastic cup and basin

• Protective gloves and glasses

• Baking soda (to clean acid stains)

The technician should always have spare parts on hand for repairing various parts of the system (fluorescent tubes, switches, etc.) and various components such as fuses, extra cable and petroleum jelly.

15. For further information

Reference books:

- **Universal Technical Standard for Solar Home Systems**, Programme Thermie B: SUP-995-96, Commission Européenne, 1999, Fondation Energies pour le Monde, 146 rue de l'Université, 75007 Paris, France.

- **Decentralized rural electrification, an opportunity for mankind, techniques for the planet**, Christophe de Gouvello and Yves Maigne, 2000, Systèmes Solaires, 146 rue de l'Université, 75007 Paris, France. ISBN 2-913620-06-X.

- **Rural lighting, A guide for development workers**, J.P. Louineau, 180 pages, 1994, Intermediate Technology Publications, United Kingdom. ISBN 1-85339-200-6.

- **Solar Electricity, a practical guide for designing and installing small photovoltaïc systems**, Simon Roberts, 434 pages, 1991, Prentice Hall International, 66 Wood Lane End, Hemel Hempstead, Hertfordshire HP2 4RG, United Kingdom. ISBN 0-13-8263114-0.

- **Training Videos: The Installation of Small Solar Systems and The Use and Maintenance of Small Solar Systems**, Jean-Paul Louineau, VHS or CD-Rom formats, and in English and French, 2002, Alliance Soleil, 38, rue des Barrénies, 85270 Saint Hilaire de Riez, France.

- **Drinking water supply with photovoltaic pump**, H. Bonneviot, 48 pages, 2005, Systèmes Solaires, 146 rue de l'Université, 75007 Paris, France. ISBN: 2-913620-34-5.

Internet sites:
Given the development of internet cafés even in rural areas, it is becoming easier to find pertinent information about solar energy systems. Many PV manufacturers and suppliers provide information on the internet which is regularly updated.

Before using information found on the internet, it is wise to cross-check the information on 2 or 3 other sites to ensure the reliability of the information.

Some useful sites:

General information about solar energy systems
www.retscreen.net

Solar irradiation data for the world
http://energy.caeds.eng.uml.edu
http://eosweb.larc.nasa.gov/sse/
http://re.jrc.cec.eu.int/pvgis/pv/countries/countries.htm

16. Glossary

AC	Alternating current (230 Volts AC is the voltage provided by most mains electricity supplies, although sometimes at 115 Volts).
Adapter DC/DC	Electrical appliance that lowers the voltage of direct current (from 12 to 6 V for example).
Ampere (A)	Unit that measures the intensity of a current (flow of electricity).
Ammeter	Apparatus which measures the intensity of current.
Auto-discharge (in %/month)	The percentage of the battery's nominal capacity lost naturally while the battery is at rest.
Automatic detection of loads (inverter)	Automatic detection feature helps to reduce energy consumption on stand-by when no loads are connected.
Battery voltage (at rest, open circuit)	The resting voltage of a battery depends on the specific gravity of the electrolyte (Pockert's law): If d = 1.24, then U = 1.24 + 0.854 = 2.085; 2.085 x 6 = 12.51 V If d = 1.28, then U = 1.28 + 0.854 = 2.134; 2.134 x 6 = 12.80 V
By-pass diode	Diode pairs often installed by manufacturers in the junction boxes of PV modules, they avoid damage to a shaded cell (for example, shaded by leaves or large bird dropping).
C/100 (capacity)	Capacity of a battery over 100 hours. For example, a 75 Ah battery C/100 can produce a current of 0.75A for 100 hours. (Capacity in C/100 = 1.25 x C/10. For example, a 120 Ah C/10 battery will have a capacity C/100 of: 1.25 x 120 = 150 Ah).
Cell temperature	This is the temperature of the cells inside a PV module. It is usually between 40 and 50°C at noon, on sunny days. The higher the temperature, the greater the loss of power of the module.
Cells (battery)	A 12 V battery is comprised of 6 independent 2 V cells.
Cells (photovoltaic)	Semi-conductor that converts the suns rays into DC electricity.

Cycle (Cycle life)	A cycle refers to a charge and a discharge of a battery. The cycle life of a battery corresponds to the number of cycles it can support before losing more than 20% of its nominal capacity definitively.
Daily depth of discharge (DDOD)	The ratio of the usable capacity to the rated capacity of a battery, or the degree of discharge that a battery can support daily (for example, if the daily energy needs are 20 Ah, the DDOD of a 100 Ah battery will be 20%).
DC	Direct current (it is in this form that electricity is stored in a battery).
Deep discharge	A discharge of more than 50% of the capacity of the battery. For example, 50 Ah for a 100 Ah battery. Deep discharges reduce the lifespan of a battery and are to be avoided.
Distilled water	A vented battery consumes distilled water. Distilled water is pure water that can be purchased from battery suppliers (the bottles should be clearly labelled and with a tamper-proof cap). Rain water is also distilled water of good quality, but only under certain conditions: - Collect rainwater directly into a clean, plastic basin. Rainwater collected from a metal roof is no longer pure or distilled. - Store the rainwater in a sealable glass or plastic bottle. Never store distilled water in a metal recipient, it will lose its purity.
Efficiency (energy)	Ratio of the output energy to input energy of a given appliance. It is always less than 1 (for example, 0.75 to 0.90 for an inverter).
Electrolyte	Mixture of sulphuric acid and pure water contained in a lead-acid battery.
Equalisation charge	Complimentary charge applied for 5 to 7 hours to a battery already charged. The charge current should be about C/20 (for example, 5 A for a 100 Ah battery). Equalisation threshold is usually higher than the standard one.
Forced charge (found on certain regulators)	Automatic charge which allows for a higher charge threshold (for example, 14.9 V) each time the regulator cuts off at low voltage. This is recommended for vented batteries.

Formatting (initial charge)	The initial full charge of a battery that formats the plates and increases the lifespan of the battery. To be carried out before putting it into service.
Inverter DC/AC	Device that converts direct current (DC) into alternating current (AC).
Irradiance	Instantaneous solar power on a given surface (for example, 1000 W/m²).
Junction box (solar module)	Box found on the back of a solar module where the cables are attached.
kWh/m²/day	Unit of measurement of solar energy received on a surface of one square metre per day.
LED	Light Emitting Diode, may vary in colour: green, yellow, red or white.
Light efficiency	The capacity of a bulb/lamp to produce light (lm/W). It is also called: luminous efficacy.
Market price	Average sale prices of goods on a local or national market.
Maximal depth of discharge (DOD)	The maximum amount of nominal battery capacity that can be used. This depends on the technology of the battery. For example, DOD is 70% for a stationary battery and only 30% for a car battery.
Multimeter	An apparatus which measures current, voltage and electrical resistance in DC and AC.
Nominal capacity of a battery (in Ah)	The amount of electricity stored in a battery under a given set of conditions (rate of discharge, temperature and end of discharge voltage).
Open circuit voltage	Voltage of a system (for example, a battery, a PV module) when it is disconnected from all electrical circuits.
Overcharge (battery)	The act of continuing to charge a battery even though it is already charged, with the consequence of reducing its lifespan.
Overcharge (circuit)	A larger amount of current passing through a cable than that for which it was designed (for example, the addition of several appliances on one socket, without verifying the size of the cables).
Power factor (cos φ)	Valid for appliances in AC ($P = U \times I \times \cos \varphi$). Cos φ is equal to 0.7 for most TVs, radios and small electric motors.
Pp (Wp)	Peak power of a PV module expressed in Wp.

Plates (battery)	A battery consists of plates of lead and lead oxide. The construction of these plates (for example, flat or tubular) has a strong influence on its lifespan.
PV array	Two or more PV modules connected together.
PV module	A number of PV cells connected and mounted together in a sealed, weatherproof unit, generally covered with a plate of glass.
PV (Photovoltaic)	Relates to devices that directly convert daylight into electricity.
PWM (Pulse with modulation)	PWM is often used as one method of charging. Instead of a steady output from the relay controller, it sends out a series of short charging pulses to the battery - a very rapid 'on-off' switch. The controller constantly checks the state of the battery to determine how fast to send pulses, and how long (wide) the pulses will be. In a fully charged battery with no load, it may just 'tick' every few seconds and send a short pulse to the battery. In a discharged battery, the pulses would be very long and almost continuous, or the controller may go into 'full on' mode.
Quasi sinus	Type of electric signal from a low quality inverter. An inverter with a 'quasi-sinus' may cause interferences with FM radios. Preference should be given to 'pure sinusoid' inverters (better efficiency, but more expensive).
Rate of discharge	This is the discharge current expressed as a fraction of the nominal capacity of the battery (for example, C/100 for a 100 Ah battery gives a discharge current of 1 A, and C/10 a current of 10 A).
Remote control (inverter)	This system allows an inverter to be connected directly to the battery and its control circuit to the regulator which will pilot it (to protect the battery against deep discharges). Contact solar suppliers for more information about such systems, generally installed on inverters greater than 400 W.
Resistance (Ohm)	Measure of how well electricity is conducted in a circuit.
Sealed battery	Battery having no access to the electrolyte inside, no caps to remove. The electrolyte is in gel form inside.
Short-circuit current (Isc)	Current measured when the two poles of a PV module are connected to a multimeter or an ammeter. Only PV panels can be short-circuited (never short-circuit a battery!).

Sinusoid	Type of alternating current (AC) that is supplied by mains electricity.
Solar battery	Battery similar in aspect to a car battery, but with thicker plates for a longer lifespan. They can be sealed or vented.
Specific gravity (electrolyte)	The specific gravity refers to the concentration of acid in the electrolyte. The specific gravity is low (for example, 1.100) when the battery is discharged and higher when the battery is charged (for example, 1.240). Specific gravity decreases as temperature rises at a rate of -0.0007/°C (for example, 1.227 at 20°C and 1.220 at 30°C).
Stationary battery	Battery with tubular plates, a large reservoir of electrolyte and often with a transparent casing. 12 V unit (monobloc) or 2 V cell. They can be vented or sealed.
Stand-by consumption (mode)	Power consumed by certain electrical appliances (for example, inverters, TV) when they are plugged in but not in use.
Sulphatation (sulphated battery)	Phenomenon appearing in old batteries and those left in a state of under-charge for several weeks. Such a battery has a strong internal resistance. When a current is applied, its voltage rises rapidly to cross the end of charge regulation threshold of the regulator, whereas only a small amount of current has been stored.
Temperature compensation (regulator)	Feature on a regulator that automatically decreases the end of charge threshold to compensate for temperature increases.
Varistors	Electronic component that protects a regulator from lightning surges.
Vented battery	Battery that has orifices for filling.
Volt (V)	Unit that measures voltage.
Voltmeter	Apparatus that measures voltage.
Watt (W)	Unit that measures electric power.
Watt/m²	Unit that measures irradiance (power received from the sun per unit area).
Watt peak (Wp)	Unit that measures the maximum power produced by a PV module.
Watt-hour (Wh)	Unit that measures energy.

17. Annexes

EXAMPLE OF A SIMPLIFIED SIZING PROCEDURE OF A PHOTOVOLTAIC INSTALLATION

Type of system: Small DC lighting system

Date: 17 / 06 / 2008

Technician name: Justin Diatta

Site reference: Affiniam

Client: private owner, Mr. Badji

Full address: Affiniam, district of Bignona

Exact installation location: Main house

1. ENERGY NEEDS OF THE CLIENT

DESCRIPTION OF APPLIANCES (list first the DC appliances, then the AC ones)	INDICATE DC OR AC ACCORDING TO APPLIANCE	LOCATION	QTY	NOMINAL POWER (W)	DURATION OF USE (hours/day)	EFFICIENCY*	ENERGY CONSUMPTION (Wh/day)	MAXIMUM CURRENT IN DC (A) **
Fluorescent lamp, 12 V	DC	kitchen	1	X 8	X 2	/ 1	= 16	0.67
Fluorescent lamp, 12 V	DC	main room	1	X 8	X 4	/ 1	= 32	0.67
Fluorescent lamp, 12 V	DC	bedroom	1	X 8	X 2	/ 1	= 16	0.67
Small radio 3 V, including power adapter, 5 W	DC	main room	1	X 5	X 3	/ 1	= 15	0.42
				X	X	/	=	
				X	X	/	=	

* For DC appliances, take the value 1; For AC appliances, indicate the inverter efficiency choose a value between 0.70 and 0.90)

** DC current = Nominal power of each appliance / (inverter efficiency x U batt)

Total needs Nd (Wh/day)	79	2.42
System voltage (V)	12 V
Total Needs in (Ah)	6.58 Ah

2. SOLAR ARRAY SIZING

Peak Power Pp = Nd / (Eb x Ei x IRR)

Eb: charge / discharge efficiency of the batteries

Ei: energy efficiency of the installation (takes into account high module temperature, charge regulator efficiency…)

IRR: mean daily irradiation of the worst month in the plane of the PV array (kWh/m²/day)

TOTAL NEEDS Nd (Wh/day)		Eb		Ei		IRR	PEAK POWER (Wp)	QTY OF MODULES (Nm)
79	/	0.7	/	0.85	/	4.5	29.5	1
								X
				Peak power per module Ppu (Wp):				32
								=
(Note: Eb x Ei = 0.6)				Installed Peak Power Pp (Wp):				32

3. BATTERY SIZING

Battery Nominal Capacity = (Nd x Aut) / (DOD x U)

Aut: storage autonomy in days, 1 to 8 depending on number of consecutive days without sunshine; one can take 3 days for domestic PV systems (lighting TV, radio, etc.)

U: Battery voltage (often 12 V or 24 V)

DOD: authorised maximum depth of discharge, one can choose 50 to 70% for dedicated solar batteries and only 30% for automotive batteries

Total Needs Nd (Wh)		Aut		DOD		U batt		Nominal Capacity (Ah)	Chosen Capacity (Ah)
79	X	3	/	0.3	/	12	=	65.8	65

The chosen capacity must be higher than the minimum capacity and will depend upon available battery size on the market

4. CHOICE OF REGULATOR

The regulator has to withstand at least:

- The maximum short-circuit current produced by the PV array

- The maximum current drawn by the DC appliances connected to the regulator:

$$\frac{1.9}{2.42}$$ (A) (A)

> **Sizing should be approved by the supplier whenever possible**

5. CABLE SIZING METHOD

The maximum voltage drop between battery and any appliance should be less than 0.45 V (12 V DC circuit)

Voltage drop = Lc x R x I

Lc: length of two core cable (for example: between regulator and one appliance)

I: Current passing through the cable

Cable size in mm²	1	1.5	2.5	4	6	10	16
Resistance (Ohm / meter) (R)	0.04	0.0274	0.01642	0.01018	0.00678	0.0039	0.00248

Example calculation: Voltage drop in a 15 m long cable, size 2.5 mm², powering a lamp of 8 W (12 V - 0.6 A); Voltage drop = 15 x 0.01642 x 0.6 = 0.15 V

Example calculation: Voltage drop in a 3 meter long cable, size 4 mm², powering a 200 W / 24 V - 220 V inverter; voltage drop = 3 x 0.01018 x 200/24 = 0.25 V

6. SIZING RATIO FOR DOUBLE-CHECKING

Daily depth of discharge (DDOD): Nd (Ah/day) / (Chosen capacity (Ah)): $\boxed{0.10}$ should always be less than DOD/AUT

Ratio: (Ppu x Nm x IRR x Ei x Eb) / Nd: $\boxed{1.08}$ should always be greater than 1

Ratio: Chosen capacity / (Isc x Nm) $\boxed{34.21}$ should be between 20 and 40

EXAMPLE OF A SIMPLIFIED SIZING PROCEDURE OF AN INSTALLATION WITH AN INVERTER

Type of system: *Lighting and audiovisual*	Site reference: *Koumatou*
Date: 19 / 06 / 2008	Client: *private owner, Mr Traouré Kanté*
Technician name: *Djibrill et Jeff Yogho Andona*	Full address: *Village of Kuly*
	Exact installation location: *Main house*

Reason for the use of an inverter:

The client owned recent AC appliances and did not want to change them for DC ones.

1. ENERGY NEEDS OF THE CLIENT

DESCRIPTION OF APPLIANCES (list first the DC appliances, then the AC ones)	INDICATE DC OR AC ACCORDING TO APPLIANCE	LOCATION	QTY		NOMINAL POWER (W)		DURATION OF USE (hours/ day)		EFFICIENCY*		ENERGY CONSUMPTION (Wh/day)	MAXIMUM CURRENT IN DC (A) **
Fluorescent lamp, 12 V	DC	kitchen	1	X	8	X	4	/	1	=	32	0.67
Fluorescent lamp, 12 V	DC	main room	1	X	13	X	5	/	1	=	65	1.08
Fluorescent lamp, 12 V	DC	bedroom	1	X	8	X	3	/	1	=	24	0.67
Small radio 3 V, including power adapter, 5 W	DC	main room	1	X	17	X	4	/	1	=	68	1.42
Colour TV 50W, 230 V	AC	main room	1	X	50	X	4	/	0.7	=	286	5.95
VCR 20 W, 230 V	AC	main room	1	X	20	X	2	/	0.7	=	57.1	2.38

* For DC appliances, take the value 1; For AC appliances, indicate the inverter efficiency (choose a value between 0.70 and 0.90)

** DC current = Nominal power of each appliance / (inverter efficiency x U batt)

Total needs Nd (Wh/day)	532	12.17
System voltage (V)		12 V
Total Needs in (Ah)		44.32 Ah

2. SOLAR ARRAY SIZING

Peak Power Pp = Nd / (Eb x Ei x IRR)

Eb: charge / discharge efficiency of the batteries

Ei: energy efficiency of the installation (takes into account high module temperature, charge regulator efficiency…)

IRR: mean daily irradiation of the worst month in the plane of the PV array (kWh/m²/day)

TOTAL NEEDS Nd (Wh/day)		Eb		Ei		IRR		PEAK POWER (Wp)	QTY OF MODULES (Nm)
532	/	0.7	/	0.85	/	4.5		198.6	4
									X
						Peak power per module Ppu (Wp):			50
									=
(Note: Eb x Ei = 0.6)						Installed Peak Power Pp (Wp):			200

3. BATTERY SIZING

Battery Nominal Capacity = (Nd x Aut) / (DOD x U)

Aut: storage autonomy in days, 1 to 8 depending on number of consecutive days without sunshine; one can take 3 days for domestic PV systems (lighting TV, radio, etc.)

U: Battery voltage (often 12 V or 24 V)

DOD: authorised maximum depth of discharge, one can choose 50 to 70% for dedicated solar batteries and only 30% for automotive batteries

Total Needs Nd (Wh)		Aut		DOD		U batt		Nominal Capacity (Ah)	Chosen Capacity (Ah)
532	X	3	/	0.5	/	12	=	265.9	270

The chosen capacity must be higher than the minimum capacity and will depend upon available battery size on the market

4. CHOICE OF REGULATOR

The regulator has to withstand at least:

- The maximum short-circuit current produced by the PV array   12.2 (A)

- The maximum current drawn by the DC appliances connected to the regulator: 12.17 (A)

> **Sizing should be approved by the supplier whenever possible**

5. CABLE SIZING METHOD

The maximum voltage drop between battery and any appliance should be less than 0.45 V (12 V DC circuit)

Voltage drop = Lc x R x I

Lc: length of two core cable (for example: between regulator and one appliance)

I: Current passing through the cable

Cable size in mm^2	1	1.5	2.5	4	6	10	16
Resistance (Ohm / meter) (R)	0.04	0.0274	0.01642	0.01018	0.00678	0.0039	0.00248

Example calculation: Voltage drop in a 15 m long cable, size 2.5 mm^2, powering a lamp of 8 W (12 V - 0.6 A); Voltage drop = 15 x 0.01642 x 0.6 = 0.15 V

Example calculation: Voltage drop in a 3 meter long cable, size 4 mm^2, powering a 200 W / 24 V - 220 V inverter; voltage drop = 3 x 0.01018 x 200/24 = 0.25 V

6. SIZING RATIO FOR DOUBLE-CHECKING

Daily depth of discharge (DDOD): Nd (Ah/day) / (Chosen capacity (Ah)):   0.16   should always be less than DOD/AUT

Ratio: (Ppu x Nm x IRR x Ei x Eb) / Nd: 1.01   should always be greater than 1

Ratio: Chosen capacity / (Isc x Nm)   22.13   should be between 20 and 40

SIMPLIFIED SIZING PROCEDURE FORM

Type of system: _____ Site reference: _____ Reason for the use of an inverter:

Date: _____ Client: _____ _____

Technician name: _____ Full address: _____ _____

Exact installation location: _____

1. ENERGY NEEDS OF THE CLIENT

DESCRIPTION OF APPLIANCES (list first the DC appliances, then the AC ones)	INDICATE DC OR AC ACCORDING TO APPLIANCE	LOCATION	QTY		NOMINAL POWER (W)		DURATION OF USE (hours/ day)		EFFICIENCY*		ENERGY CONSUMPTION (Wh/day)	MAXIMUM CURRENT IN DC (A) **
				X		X		/		=		
				X		X		/		=		
				X		X		/		=		
				X		X		/		=		
				X		X		/		=		
				X		X		/		=		

For DC appliances, take the value 1; For AC appliances, indicate the inverter efficiency (choose a value between 0.70 and 0.90)

** DC current = Nominal power of each appliance / (inverter efficiency x U batt)*

Total needs Nd (Wh/day) _____

System voltage (V) _____

Total Needs in (Ah)

2. SOLAR ARRAY SIZING

Peak Power Pp = Nd / (Eb x Ei x IRR)

Eb: charge / discharge efficiency of the batteries

Ei: energy efficiency of the installation (takes into account high module temperature, charge regulator efficiency…)

IRR: mean daily irradiation of the worst month in the plane of the PV array (kWh/m²/day)

TOTAL NEEDS Nd (Wh/day)		Eb		Ei		IRR		PEAK POWER (Wp)	QTY OF MODULES (Nm)
	/	0.7	/	0.85	/				
									X
			Peak power per module Ppu (Wp):						
									=
(Note: Eb x Ei = 0.6)			Installed Peak Power Pp (Wp):						

3. BATTERY SIZING

Battery Nominal Capacity = (Nd x Aut) / (DOD x U)

Aut: storage autonomy in days, 1 to 8 depending on number of consecutive days without sunshine; one can take 3 days for domestic PV systems (lighting TV, radio, etc.)

U: Battery voltage (often 12 V or 24 V)

DOD: authorised maximum depth of discharge, one can choose 50 to 70% for dedicated solar batteries and only 30% for automotive batteries

Total Needs Nd (Wh)		Aut		DOD		U batt		Nominal Capacity (Ah)	Chosen Capacity (Ah)
	x		/		/		=		

The chosen capacity must be higher than the minimum capacity and will depend upon available battery size on the market

4. CHOICE OF REGULATOR

The regulator has to withstand at least:

- The maximum short-circuit current produced by the PV array   (A)

- The maximum current drawn by the DC appliances connected to the regulator: (A)

> **Sizing should be approved by the supplier whenever possible**

5. CABLE SIZING METHOD

The maximum voltage drop between battery and any appliance should be less than 0.45 V (12 V DC circuit)

Voltage drop = Lc x R x I

Lc: length of two core cable (for example: between regulator and one appliance)

I: Current passing through the cable

Cable size in mm²	1	1.5	2.5	4	6	10	16
Resistance (Ohm / meter) (R)	0.04	0.0274	0.01642	0.01018	0.00678	0,0039	0.00248

Example calculation: Voltage drop in a 15 m long cable, size 2.5 mm², powering a lamp of 8 W (12 V - 0.6 A), Voltage drop = 15 x 0.01642 x 0.6 = 0.15 V

Example calculation: Voltage drop in a 3 meter long cable, size 4 mm², powering a 200 W / 24 V - 220 V inverter; voltage drop = 3 x 0.01018 x 200/24 = 0.25 V

6. SIZING RATIO FOR DOUBLE-CHECKING

Daily depth of discharge (DDOD): Nd (Ah/day) / (Chosen capacity (Ah)):   should always be less than DOD/AUT

Ratio: (Ppu x Nm x IRR x Ei x Eb) / Nd: should always be greater than 1

Ratio: Chosen capacity / (Isc x Nm)   should be between 20 and 40

EXAMPLE OF A QUOTATION FOR AN INSTALLATION

Type of system: Small DC lighting system

Site reference: Affiniam

Date: 17 / 06 / 2008

Client: private owner, Mr. Badji

Technician name: Justin Diatta

Full address: Affiniam, district of Bignona

Exact installation location: House

1. LIST OF COMPONENTS

Description of apparatus (Make, type, power, input voltage, …)	Quantity		Unit cost (€)		Total cost (€)
Module 32 Wp, monocristalline	1	X	225.00	=	225.00
Module structure	1	X	19.50	=	19.50
Two core cable H07RNF 2 x 2.5 mm² (meter)	5	X	1.30	=	6.50
Charge regulator XR8-12 V / 6 A with user notice	1	X	32.00	=	32.00
Two core cable H05VVF 2 x 4 mm² (meter)	2	X	1.50	=	3.00
Battery 65 Ah, 12 V (automotive type)	1	X	55.00	=	55.00
Electrolyte (litre)	5	X	0.50	=	2.50
Fluorescent lamp 8 W, 12 V	3	X	16.00	=	48.00
Adapter DC/DC, 12 V / 6 V	1	X	9.00	=	9.00
Two core cable H05VVF 2 x 2.5 mm² (meter)	30	X	0.70	=	21.00
Junction box	4	X	1.00	=	4.00
Unipolar switch 10 A	3	X	3.50	=	10.50
Socket with earth pole 12 V (male and female)	1	X	12.00	=	12.00
Fuse holder and fuse 5 A	2	X	4.00	=	8.00
Cable tie, number (box of 100 units)	2	X	10.00	=	20.00
Wood screw, 4/35	30	X	0.02	=	0.60
Connexion bar of 10 'dominos', black 4 mm	1	X	1.50	=	1.50
Connexion bar of 10 'dominos', black 10 mm	1	X	1.00	=	1.00
Wall plug Diameter 8 mm	30	X	0.02	=	0.60
Battery box	1	X	10.00	=	10.00
Distilled water (litre)	1	X	0.50	=	0.50
			TOTAL COMPONENT COSTS:		490.20 (a)

	(b)%		
- Unforeseen expenses (a percentage of total component cost)	5	24.51	(c) = (a) x (b)
Total cost of system components		514.71	(d) = (a) + (c)

2. INSTALLATION COSTS

- Transportation (from your workshop to the installation site)		25.00	
- Labour (number of technicians x daily salary cost x number of days)	2 X 15 X 1.5 =	45.00	
- Other costs (lodging,...)		15.00	
Total cost of system components		85.00	(e)

3. TOTAL COST PRICE OF THE SYSTEM

Cost price	599.71	(f) = (d) + (e)

4. SALE PRICE OF THE INSTALLATION

(Sale price = cost price x% of margin)

	(g)%	(h)	
- Your margin (should be between 15 and 25%)	20	119.94	(h) = (g) x (f)
Your minimum sale price		719.65	(f) + (h)

OPTION

Annual maintenance visit, including transport to site	25.00

Remark: Once you have sold the system, try to reduce all your costs: try to purchase cheaper components of the same quality. The suppliers may offer you better prices if you buy in large quantities and if you keep doing business with them.

Annex 5

QUOTATION PROCEDURE FORM

Type of system: _____   Site reference: _____

Date: _____   Client: _____

Technician name: _____   Full address: _____

   Exact installation location: _____

1. LIST OF COMPONENTS

DESCRIPTION OF APPARATUS (MAKE, TYPE, POWER, INPUT VOLTAGE, ...)	QUANTITY		UNIT COST (€)		TOTAL COST (€)
		X		=	
		X		=	
		X		=	
		X		=	
		X		=	
		X		=	
		X		=	
		X		=	
		X		=	
		X		=	
		X		=	
		X		=	
		X		=	
		X		=	
		X		=	
		X		=	
		X		=	
		X		=	
		X		=	
		X		=	
		X		=	
			TOTAL COMPONENT COSTS:		(a)

	(b)%		
- Unforeseen expenses (a percentage of total component cost)			(c) = (a) x (b)
Total cost of system components			(d) = (a) + (c)

2. INSTALLATION COSTS

- Transportation (from your workshop to the installation site)			
- Labour (number of technicians x daily salary cost x number of days)	... x ... x ... =		
- Other costs (lodging,...)			
Total cost of system components		(e)	

3. TOTAL COST PRICE OF THE SYSTEM

Cost price		(f) = (d) + (e)

4. SALE PRICE OF THE INSTALLATION

(Sale price = cost price x% of margin)

	(g)%	(h)	
- Your margin (should be between 15 and 25%)			(h) = (g) x (f)
Your minimum sale price			(f) + (h)

OPTION

Annual maintenance visit, including transport to site

Remark: Once you have sold the system, try to reduce all your costs: try to purchase cheaper components of the same quality. The suppliers may offer you better prices if you buy in large quantities and if you keep doing business with them.

USER NOTICE FOR YOUR SOLAR SYSTEM

Your system can operate the following appliances for a limited period each day:

TYPE	LOCATION	MAXIMUM DURATION OF DAILY USE
Lamp 8 W	Kitchen	3 hours
Lamp 8 W	Bedroom	2 hours
Lamp 8 W	Main room	4 hours
Radio-cassette	Main room	5 hours

- **Respect the maximum duration of use for each appliance listed above.**

- **Switch off appliances (lamps, radio, etc.) and the inverter when not in use.**

- **Monitor the regulator indicators regularly.**

Monthly maintenance

> Check the level of electrolyte in the battery, add DISTILLED WATER if required.
NEVER ADD ORDINARY WATER OR ACID.

> Ensure that the battery connectors are tight and clean.

> Clean the solar modules with clean water and a soft cloth.

> Keep the modules free from any surrounding shade.

> Never put anything on the surface of the modules.

WARNING!

*Keep your solar system clean
and
Do not add any extra appliances
without asking your solar technician*

In case of problem, contact us:

 CAREFUL USER = LONG LASTING SYSTEM

System installed by: .... installation date: ....